THE NIKON IMAGE

a collection
of contemporary
photographic art from
17 of today's greatest
photographers

Library of Congress catalog card number: 74-33149

This book was designed and produced by
Gilbert, Felix & Sharf, Inc. 566 7th Ave., New York City, N.Y.

Art Director-Designer: Roy Tuck
Editor: Ed Rooney

Printed and bound in the United States by
The Case-Hoyt Corporation, Rochester, N.Y.

THE NIKON IMAGE

CONTENTS

The Nikon Image was conceived out of a desire on our part to provide a lasting showcase for the more serious artistic work being produced by outstanding photographers. For us, this book is a logical extension of our dedication and involvement with photography.

The seventeen photographers whose work appears on the following pages encompass a great many styles and approaches. The thinking behind their images sometimes varies greatly. Perhaps their only common denominator is the Nikon camera. That, and an abundance of talent and visual sensitivity.

These are the modern masters of the still image. Some are already legendary names in the medium. Men like Art Kane, PeteTurner, Jay Maisel, Douglas Kirkland and John Dominis, have long since established their reputations. The sheer weight of the outstanding work they have produced over the years is awesome.

Then there are the young lions—Mitchell Funk, John Lawlor, Eric Meola, George Obremski and Ken Biggs. The names may not be as instantly familiar, at least not yet, but anyone who looks at magazines has come across their innovative and imaginative images.

The portfolios begin with a verbal self-portrait as well as a photographic self-portrait. In order to explore the philosophy of each photographer and the reasons for his involvement with the medium, we talked with each one at length, with the aid of a tape recorder. In this way, we hoped to bring forth informative glimpses of the men behind the photographs.

In addition, the photographers have been most helpful in providing an unusually precise and detailed explanation of how each picture was made. For the serious camera enthusiast, these pages on technique provide a rare opportunity to look over the shoulders of these leading contemporary photographers and learn exactly how they go about building an image.

We would like to offer our sincere thanks to each and every one of the seventeen photographers whose work appears within. They took time out from their busy schedules and cooperated to the fullest. Putting the book together was a most gratifying experience. It's always rewarding to work hand-in-hand with photography's most creative talents, sharing their needs and sharing their successes. This close liaison, over the years, with the world's leading professionals has helped us greatly in fulfilling our own deep commitment to the medium. At Nikon, we are proud to feel that we've shared in the creating of all the images in this volume.

morton beebe

I've always been motivated to travel by an interest in people and the things that make them different, their philosophies and customs. What I'm trying to do in photography is capture some of these differences, the subtleties that separate one group of people from another.

It's no longer necessary to work with a brush and canvas and pigment to be considered an artist. The camera is an art medium as well. The picture has become almost as important as the reality. Seeing a person in print or on a screen can seem more meaningful than confronting the same person face to face. So in a way, pictures are almost truer than life.

A person in the arts should view his past work as less important than the work he's doing today. The eye changes. Abilities and perceptions improve constantly. You should be excited about the work you're doing at the moment. I'm always looking forward to the next project.

Many people think photography is a matter of discovering the trick. But we're not magicians. Photography is like tennis: you take lessons, you learn how to use the racquet and then you begin to play the game. Playing the game is what it's all about.

KEN biGGS

The greatest pictures project a strong idea or feeling. Vague ideas don't lead to strong graphic statements. If you begin with a solid point of view that you want to express, you'll find it much easier to decide on an approach that will support that idea. I experiment with different techniques in order to find the means to express a certain mood or feeling. This is not technique for its own sake. Visual effects are like words, in that they help you articulate an idea.

In the beginning I was strongly influenced by other styles and approaches but the turning point for a photographer comes when he finds his own direction. It's like leaving the womb. At first you're a bit scared and uncertain but soon you get your creative legs under you and you're on your way.

You hear a lot of photographers talking about their dissatisfaction with the still image. They move into films because they feel that motion pictures are more creative. They'd be better off looking into themselves for creativity.

I want to direct my creative energies towards expressing the grand themes of life such as freedom, beauty, love and hope. For me, photography is the perfect art form. It frees me from boredom and involves me with life.

john dominis

The photographic essay, or picture story, is my preferred form of work. Throughout an assignment, I look for a lead photograph which contains the main information about the story, but that also makes the viewer feel the meaning emotionally. Often this picture does not suddenly appear in front of me; it has to be "made" rather than "taken." The other photographs fill out the essay and contain important information, but may not be as stimulating emotionally as that lead.

I don't have one favorite subject, but my favorite kind of assignment is one that gives me enough time to get deeply into the story so that I feel as well as understand it.

In order to express himself, it's very important for a photographer to be well grounded in his craft. It's not enough to possess talent without also possessing the ability to transfer that talent to film in exactly the way one chooses. This may mean that a great deal of equipment has to be hauled around, and countless sore shoulders endured, but in the end these technical aids become friends and accomplices.

Photography has given me a rare chance to witness great events and to look at life in many places and under many conditions. For a quarter of a century my work has been an educational experience not unlike having a fellowship to study the world.

anthony Edgeworth

Edgeworth by Edgeworth

Perfect light is something I strive for in all my pictures. I like to have a kind of mystery and drama to my lighting. My sense of lighting and color goes all the way back to the Flemish painters, the rich browns and blacks and golds. I'm a throwback to another age. To me, the only true beauty is classic beauty that has stood the test of time. I want to capture this beauty on film, the things that please my eye. Whether it's good crystal or good fabrics or whatever, it all has the same colors and the same look. It always has and it always will have. There's a patina to things when they're right. My photography is a way of reaffirming my taste.

At first I found the camera very intimidating with its precision and its beauty. But as I began to work with it and control it, I started to feel better about myself and the things around me.

People have a number of options open to them at certain times in their lives. Photography was the way I chose. I became a photographer, really, because I thought it would be nice to go over and do something like take pictures of the Dublin Horse Show and be able to make a living that way. I still think so.

MITCHELL FUNK

Funk by Funk

It's funny, up until the time I got involved in photography, I can't ever recall being aware of seeing a sunset or noticing the way light strikes things. Now the awareness of light is always with me. It's become part of me. I'm always looking at the way light plays on objects at different times of day and changes their mood.

I like to use light in combination with pure color. I'm most fascinated with monochromatic color or the combination of two strongly contrasting colors.

I'm driven to experiment. I want to go beyond the ordinary and turn common, everyday subjects into something exciting and unusual. Often I come across picture situations that don't quite make it. The germ is there but something more is needed. This is where multiple images can help. Sometimes images that are relatively tame by themselves can be added together to produce something powerful.

It should be possible for a photographer to be creative and commercial at the same time, but all too often the client wants to think of a photographer as being able to produce only one kind of picture. This business has become one of specialists and I think that's sad because many photographers can handle a number of very different kinds of jobs, and do them all well. I thrive on variety. The last thing I want to do is keep repeating a certain kind of picture over and over again just because it worked once.

FRANCISCO Hidalgo

Hidalgo by Hidalgo

I cannot explain in words what kind of photographer I am or what kind of pictures I take. I cannot say I take "creative" pictures. It means nothing. I cannot say I take "nice" pictures because that's silly. So, when people ask, I say only that I take pictures and leave it at that.

Sometimes I see something and I take the picture very fast. I don't have the right lens or film. The light is not good. So I say to myself, I'll go back and get that picture with the right lens, the right film and the right light. Everything will be perfect. But I always find that the first time was the best. The first feeling is always right.

Making photographs is, to me, like a sport. And so I've made myself a set of rules. I use filters, prisms, double exposures—anything—but always the picture must be made entirely in the camera. I make only color photography now. But I don't feel that color photography needs to have all the colors. The best color is very soft and discreet. I don't like red and blue together, for instance, because, in my eye, they clash.

It's not enough only to take pictures. A photographer today must be a connoisseur of everything; an encyclopedia of taste. There are a lot of young people with talent but today talent is not enough. One must be a genius. And what is a genius? A genius is a person with talent who works harder than anyone else.

ART KANE

I never dreamt that I'd become a photographer. As a kid, I had a friend who had his own darkroom. I would go down into his basement and look at all that equipment and chemicals and paraphernalia and it would frighten me. To this day, having too much to do with mechanical things makes me uneasy. Whatever degree of camera technique I was able to acquire over the years came to me through my naivete and playfulness. While studying at Cooper Union, I was forced to take a course in photography because it was required, and to my utter amazement I found that the camera and I got along. This was about the time that the single-lens reflex came on the scene and it appealed to me because it was small and friendly, totally unlike the cumbersome, heavy cameras that were standard in those days.

I've always considered myself an illustrator, a literate photographer interested in producing images that reflect the essence of an idea. The heros of my youth were men like N. C. Wyeth, Norman Rockwell and Maxwell Parrish, artists who illustrated stories and ideas. So when I began working with the camera, that was what I tried to do. I want to interpret the human scene rather than simply record it.

douglas Kirkland

Kirkland by Kirkland

We are in the age of the motorized miniature camera. We all must face the fact that our entire lifestyle is geared towards things moving faster and faster, so it follows that now we even have to take pictures faster. Magazines and ad agencies alike have become accustomed to the idea that work can be done more quickly. Even though the big picture magazines have now closed their doors, I still do a surprisingly large amount of editorial work, including magazine covers. Using a 35 with a motor, I can work with a subject for an hour or two and come up with the cover they want. A few years back, I might have spent a whole day.

When photographing people, you have to be totally at ease with your equipment. Because if there's a secret to this kind of shooting, it's giving your full attention to the subject. You have to be able to really listen while the subject tells you what she did the night before or what she had for lunch the other day. This may seem trivial and unimportant, but what you're doing, really, is forming a relationship. A good relationship will produce good photographs. I make sure I have all the lights and lenses I'll be needing at hand before I start the shooting. Once you're taking pictures, it should be automatic.

JOHN LAWLOR

I love being on location. I thrive on it. Maintaining a studio is like having a wife and ten children to support. I probably spend more time setting things up than I do actually taking pictures. I don't believe in jumping in and immediately beginning to shoot. I never grab stuff. It's all very planned out ahead of time. I have to arrive at some sort of idea as to what it is I'm looking for before I even load a camera. There are some happy accidents in photography but they're not really accidents because the photographer has spent years getting ready, sharpening his eye and technique.

My favorite type of job is one where I'm able to go out and shoot whatever I want as long as it's aimed at the client in question. A job like this permits the photographer to do a little bit of everything. It's far more satisfying than working from a set layout.

To me, advertising photography is an adventure. I like the coming together of a group of people who all have one particular objective in mind. Each of us makes his own individual contribution, we do the job and then go our separate ways. I find this very rewarding.

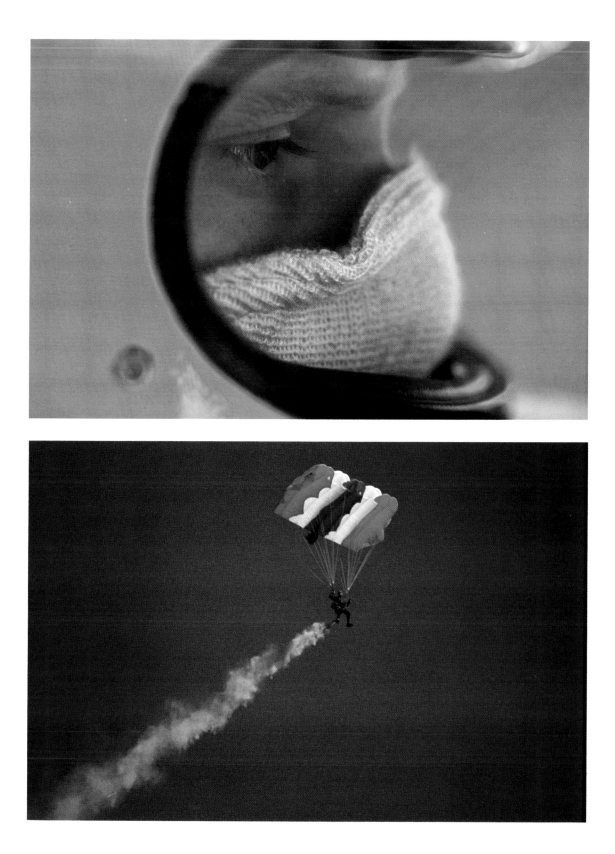

jay maisel

Maisel by Maisel

I'm trying to do something that's very much out of fashion—record beautiful images. I'm looking for those rare, fleeting moments where light and form conspire to please the eye. As a photographer, I can save these moments for loving inspection at a future time. If I'm there to observe and have enough craft to capture what's happening, I'm fine. What I end up with, hopefully, is what I started out with.

I get a tremendous kick out of what I'm doing. If I didn't, I'd do something else. My idea of a vacation is to go out and photograph. I like to take trips where I just drive, no destination, no schedule. I just get in the car in the morning and start driving. When I see something I like, I stop and take the picture.

When I'm traveling, energy is never a problem. It may be 102° in Bangkok but it's also terribly exciting because it's a place I've never been and the images are all around me. In Iran, I shot over 300 rolls of color in eight days. The fantastic exotica of the place kept me going.

I've been shooting from the roof of my building for over eight years now. That's eight years on the same subject. I go up there in all kinds of weather to record the view, the light at different times of day, and the pigeons. If I don't tire of that, I guess I'll never tire of photography.

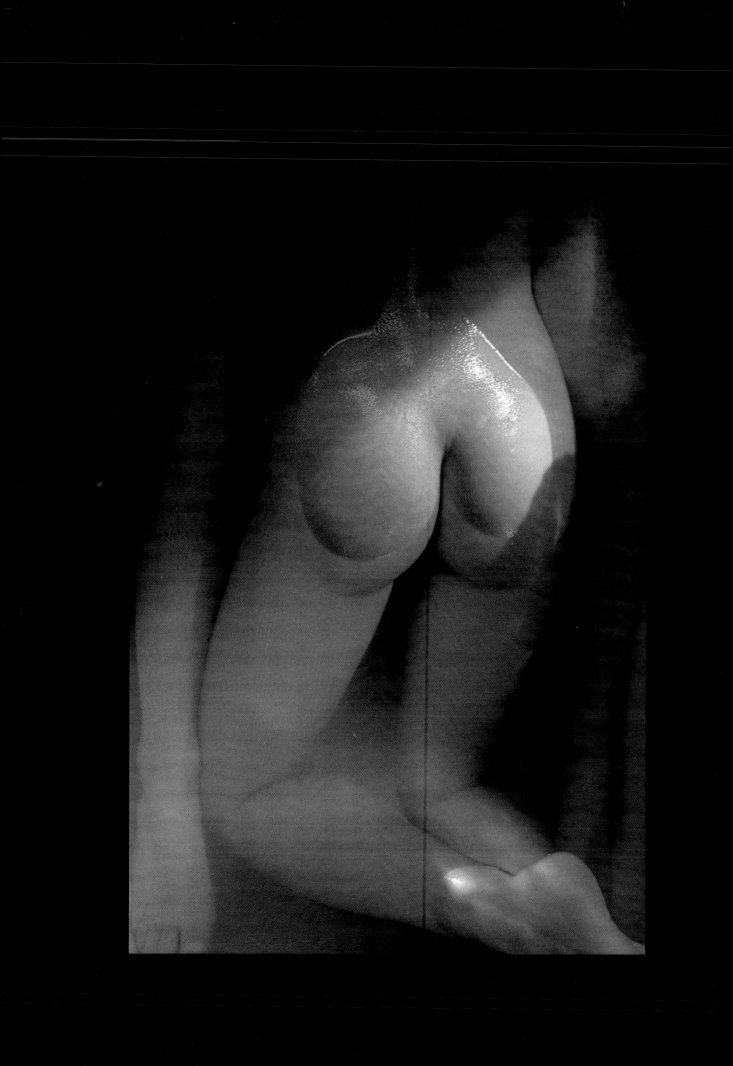

tom mccarthy

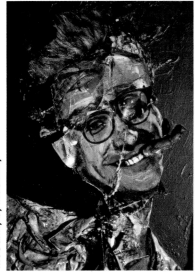

There are really no rules in photography, yet you'll always find people who will object strenuously if a picture is at all strange or different from what they're used to. Even as a kid I would try to look at things in a different way. I'd lie deep in the grass and look up at the bottoms of the flowers or climb a tree and look down through the leaves. I remember when I took my first fisheye picture into the editors of the newspaper I was working for at the time. They were livid. I mean, people had been working for centuries with square and rectangular images and here comes this "nut" with a round picture and, worse yet, a round picture full of distortion. I thought they were going to physically throw me out of the office. To give credit where it's due, they ran the picture on the front page.

Multiple exposures with infrared film are something I'm into at the moment. I like the thrill of surprise I get when I see just how close I've come to the image I had in mind. It's like the blooming of a flower. You never know exactly what it's going to look like. You only have an idea that it will turn out red or purple or blue.

Still photography seems to be headed into the area of fine art. It's hard for us to evaluate what's happening now but I think in a hundred or two hundred years people will say that we started something here. We're just poised at the beginning.

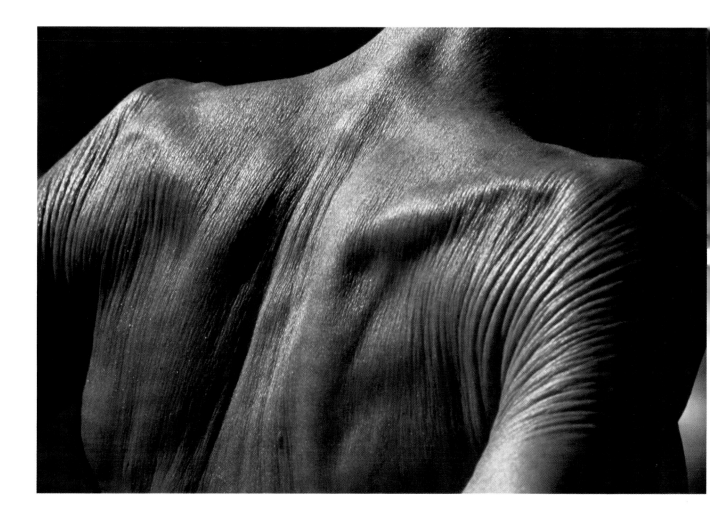

ERIC MEOLA

Photography is the only medium in which I can express myself. I'm in it because it's magic to me and this magic is what I'm trying to convey to others. I want people to turn the page of a magazine and stop. I want them to think about what photography can do rather than take it for granted.

I try to use graphics and color in the strongest possible way, to express a concept. To do this, technique is very important. What I've learned about color and filtration, for example, I've learned through a lot of trial and error and hardship on my part. Most photographers today come to color through transparency materials. I started out doing color printing in my basement when I was nineteen. I did all my experimenting with color negative materials. I believe this helped me tremendously because it gave me a basic insight into how colors interrelate and react to one another.

In the past, artists would spend all their time painting, developing new techniques, mixing colors and looking at other artists' work. They were involved. If I weren't making any money at photography, I'd still be pursuing it as intensely as I do. It's an all-consuming thing. And I think that only when it's at that level does it become an art.

GEORGE OBREMSKI

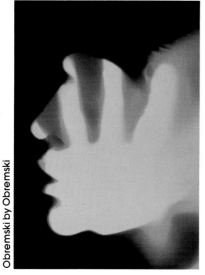

Obremski by Obremski

I never think of my work in terms of style. That would be counterproductive. When I'm shooting, I try to remain open to all possibilities. If I were to hold myself back, waiting for one particular situation to unfold, I might miss something important. There should be only one don't in photography, and that's don't restrict yourself. I take straight photographs, whatever they are, and I manipulate photographs, whatever that is. In each case, I'm striving for that ultimate image, one where all the parts come together. We're all unique. When I look at an object I see it differently than anyone else can. You work, and what you produce is what you are.

In many instances, a photograph can be produced so easily and quickly that it tends to confuse a lot of people. They come to the conclusion that photography is a simple art form. I think that a photographer should spend as much time and thought on a finished picture as a painter would spend on a painting.

Art is the product of the constant search for new ideas and new images. To be completely satisfied and content with the work you produce is death to creativity. It's the dissatisfaction that drives an artist. He must be obsessed by the idea that the image he has been striving for is on that next roll of film.

JERRY SARAPOCHIELLO

Sarapochiello by Sarapochiello

More and more I'm living inside my mind. Today, especially in the cities, people are being forced to retreat inside themselves. I don't know if that's good but it seems to be the way things are developing. It's not us any more, it's me. I believe it's these 20th-century pressures that are causing many young photographers to express themselves in Surrealistic images...images from the mind.

The things I want to say in photography are best said in a controlled environment. My work doesn't necessarily have to relate to reality. It doesn't have to be a real tree or a real mountain. I'd rather create my own mountain in the studio.

I started out as a designer and in a way I guess I'm still one, because I do design my photographs. If I have a certain idea for a picture, I sit down and draw it first. Later on it may change, but that's where I start.

Most photographers like to show groups of things. In my pictures I concentrate on one object. It's not that it's easier. I'm just drawn to a particular thing. I own most of the props I shoot. I find them here and there. I'm interested in all kinds of objects. The walls of my studio are covered with all kinds of things—antiques, natural things, even junk. Some of the objects in my photos I've had since I was a kid.

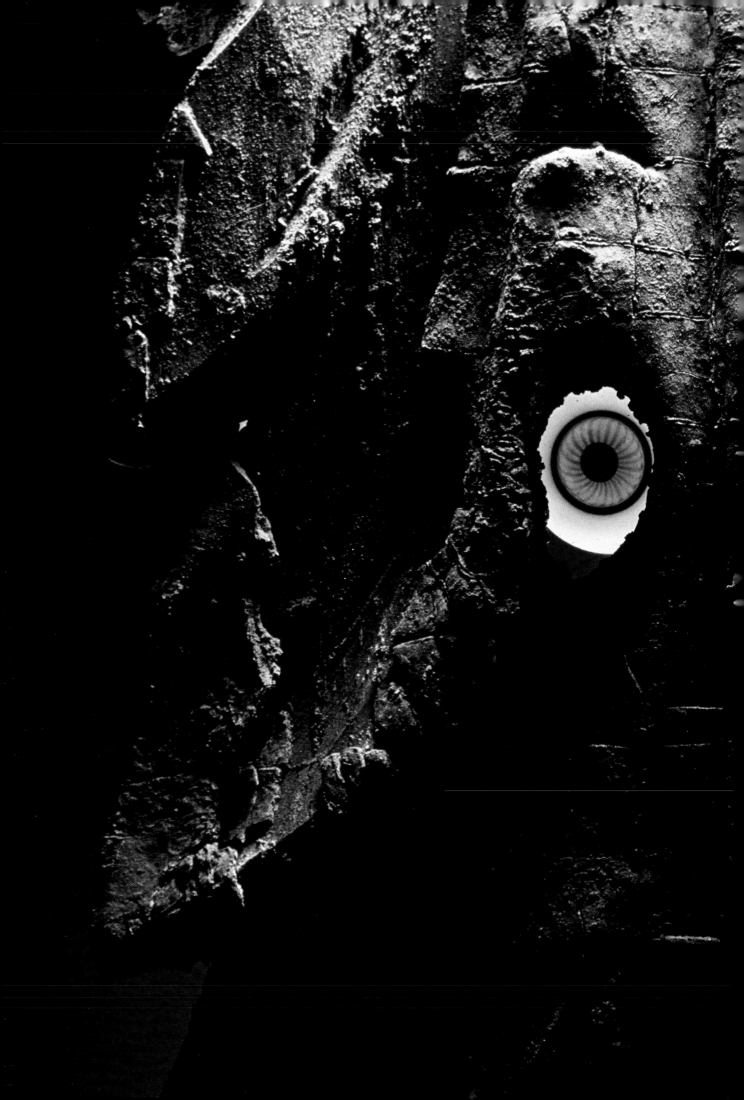

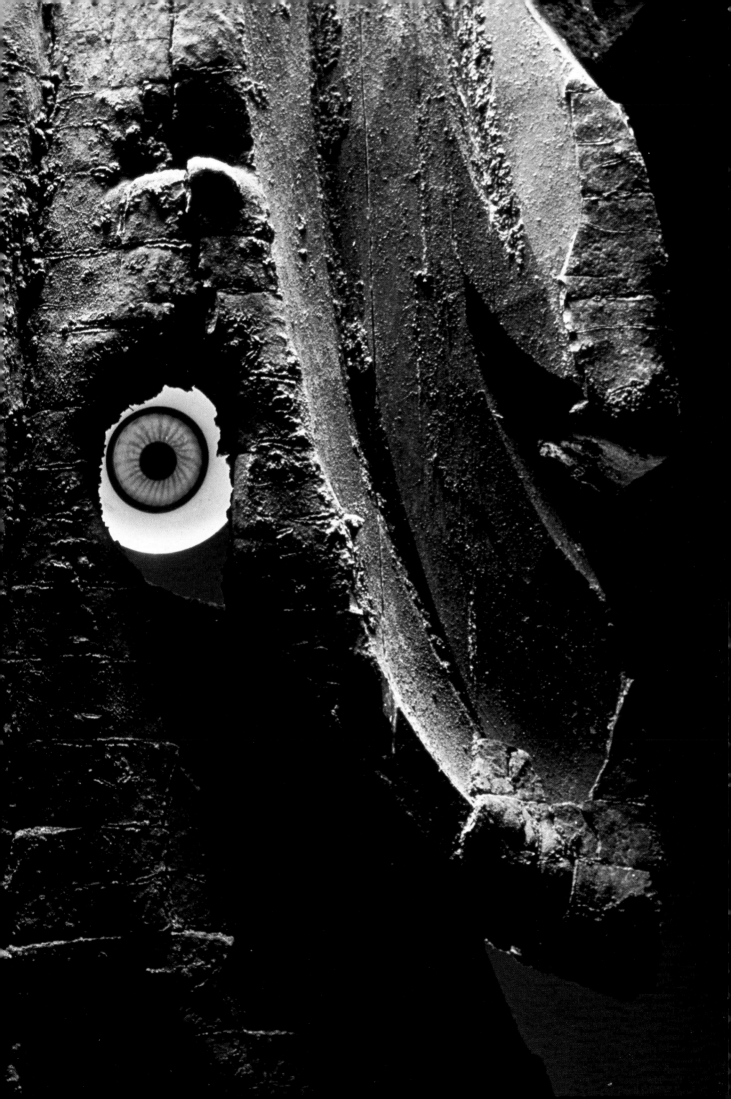

RICHARD STEEDMAN

Steedman by Steedman

Travel photographers are a special breed. Almost everything is against them, yet they persevere. The studio man leads a very organized, secure life. The wind doesn't come along and blow the food off the table while he's trying to do a still life. Rain doesn't soak his models to the skin. On location, one learns to take the most adverse conditions in stride.

I begin by studying the subject. I do this with the help of my viewfinder and a wide-angle lens. That way I can check the angle and perspective from time to time and put a frame around the subject. It's always the subject first and then whatever lens will work best on that subject, never the other way around. I carry eleven cases of equipment. I want to have whatever I need to create the picture. I don't mind traveling heavy. I don't want to have to tell anyone that I didn't go into that restaurant and get a picture of the chef because I didn't have the proper lights with me. There are no "becauses" in my business. If possible, I hire a microbus and a driver. The bus becomes my mobile studio. I see no virtue in going on location light unless you're planning to climb Mount Everest. In the field, the photographer is totally responsible for himself and the outcome of his job. Nobody is going to watch over him.

PETE TURNER

A photographer's work is given shape and style by his personal vision. It's not simply technique, but the way he looks at life and the world around him. His interests will influence his approach. I've always been an avid reader of science fiction and I think this comes through in my work.

I like to take photos that are strong in design, with super-saturated color. Color plus design. I've found, however, that I can convert my pictures to black-and-white and they still hold together. Each shot should have enough content to carry it, even without the help of strong color.

The longer you work in the medium, the more difficult it becomes to live up to your own standards because, in a way, each time you pick up the camera is the first time. You must approach each new project with a freshness and naivete. You need the enthusiasm of an amateur coupled with the skill and technique of a professional.

If another photographer is able to come up with the picture he wants after working for only an hour, while I might have to work for two days before I'm happy with the results, well, I say more power to the guy. Because in the final analysis, it's only the image that counts. How you achieve that image is immaterial.

HENRY WOLF

I solve pictorial problems. I take words and make them into pictures. In a way, you could call me a translator, because I translate English into images. In order to end up with a smooth, interesting translation, of course, one must be entirely fluent in the language of photography.

When I knew only a little about photography, I thought I knew a lot. I used to say: Who needs all these lenses? Who needs the zoom? Who needs strobe? Window light, a white background and a couple of lenses were all I needed. Now I find that approach is not enough. Some pictures require a much more involved technical solution. You go through three stages in anything that you become deeply involved with: First you're awed by the fact that it works at all, that anything comes out. Next you begin to do a few nice things and you think, this is easy, anybody can do it! Then as you get assignments and have to solve particular problems, you go back to the first stage of being intrigued by the whole technical business.

A shooting starts with a plan, an idea, and you try to cover yourself by doing what seems most logical. But once in awhile something takes over and you become part of the thing. You go into automatic pilot. That's when you know the pictures will be special.

NIKON F
200mm f4 NIKKOR
KODACHROME II
HAZE FILTER
1/500 SEC. AT f4

Deep in the jungles of New Guinea, Beebe came across this tribesman spearfishing from his dugout canoe. "The primitive simplicity of the scene struck me as being representative of the dawn of man." Beebe captured the moment from the river bank with the help of a long lens.

NIKON F
28mm f3.5 NIKKOR
KODACHROME II
1/125 SEC. AT f3.5

While documenting the daily activities of a U.S. arctic research team on Ice Island T3, Beebe found himself working under the most extreme weather conditions. The camera was kept inside his parka and only brought out briefly when he was ready to take a picture. "I didn't find it necessary to have any of my equipment specially winterized. My main problem was remembering to keep the camera away from my face because at 20° below zero metal will freeze to your skin instantly."

Beebe moved in close with a medium telephoto to fill the frame with the smiling face of this rather young bleached blonde on the South Pacific island of Guadalcanal. The medium telephoto is ideal for head shots like this because it permits the photographer to work at a comfortable distance from the subject, close enough to give instruction in a normal voice, yet far enough away so as not to intrude on personal privacy.

NIKON F
105mm f2.5 NIKKOR
KODACHROME II
1/30 SEC. AT f2.5

The extraordinary golden quality of the light in this photograph of wild horses in Australia's outback is the result of dry prairie dust rising through the rays of the early morning sun. The horses were being herded into a corral by aboriginal cowboys.

NIKON F
105mm f2.5 NIKKOR
KODACHROME II
1/125 SEC. AT f2.8

behind the images

NIKON F2
43-86mm NIKKOR ZOOM
KODACHROME II
ONE SEC. AT f5.6

Biggs focused on the color-fully lit tower of a Chinese pagoda in Copenhagen's famed Tivoli Gardens and zoomed in during the last part of his one-second ex-posure so that the lights streaked inward and con-verged at the center. "This zoom effect works best at night when the subject is a bright one surrounded by an area of darkness."

NIKON F2
105mm f2.5 NIKKOR
KODACHROME 25
CC50M FILTER
1/15 SEC. AT f5.6

This blurred-action picture was taken on a beach in southern California. Biggs placed the camera on a tripod and panned on the running figure to convey the

feeling of motion. The choice of shutter speed depends on the amount of blur desired and the speed at which the subject is traveling. Settings of 1/2 second to 1/15 second work well with people or slow-moving vehicles. A set-ting of 1/30 second works better with galloping horses, motorcycles or race cars.

NIKON F2
35mm f2 NIKKOR
KODACHROME II
80B FILTER
1/30 SEC. AT f2.8

A medium blue filter accents the cool tone of the light on a misty morning in the Red-wood Forest of northern Cal-ifornia. Biggs waited at a bend in the road till a car came along with its head-lights burning.

NIKON F2
105mm f4 BELLOWS NIKKOR
KODACHROME II
K2 FILTER
1/250 SEC. AT f4

The 105mm Nikkor bellows lens was Biggs's choice for this illustration for a vitamin manufacturer. It allowed him to solve two separate photo-graphic problems simul-taneously. "I wanted to focus in very close on the new wheat and also include a giant sun in the picture. By shooting wide open and focusing the lens on a subject that is closer than one foot away, the image of the sun distorts and expands in size as any out-of-focus bright ob-ject would." This enlarged, round sun effect is only achieved when the lens is set at its widest f-stop. If the lens had been stopped down at all, the sun would have taken on the shape of the lens diaphragm.

NIKON F
300mm f4.5 NIKKOR
EKTACHROME-X
1/250 SEC. AT f8

While producing his famous essay on Africa's big cats for Life magazine, Dominis caught the King of Beasts in a relaxed moment. The photographer was working from the back of a four-wheel drive vehicle that had been specially modified to his specifications. "Most of my shooting was done with hand-held telephotos in the 300mm to 600mm range. A tripod proved impractical because animals simply don't run in predictable straight lines. You have to stay flexible to be able to follow them when they suddenly change direction."

NIKON F2 W/MOTOR-DRIVE
300mm f4.5 NIKKOR
EKTACHROME-X
1/500 SEC. AT f8

This photograph was taken at Peking Airport during the arrival ceremony for President Nixon on the occasion of his historic first visit to Mainland China. Dominis chose a long telephoto lens in order to achieve this flat, poster-like effect. "I seem to favor long lenses. Using them for candid shots, I find, is the best way to be unobtrusive and not interfere with the natural action of a subject. I also like the tight composition they make possible and their ability to stack up subjects and isolate them from a distracting background."

NIKON F
105mm f2.5 NIKKOR
KODACHROME II
1/125 SEC. AT f4

Soft light and a medium telephoto lens were used here to capture the simple beauty of this dark-eyed child carried on her mother's back in a small village in Mexico. Dominis noticed the mother and child walking down the street near a marketplace. He walked quickly ahead and set himself in a convenient spot that had the kind of lighting he wanted, then clicked off this frame as the subject passed by.

NIKON F
600mm f5.6 NIKKOR
KODACHROME II
1/500 SEC. AT f5.6

Dominis set up his tripod on the sands of Bondi Beach in Sydney, Australia to record the maneuvers of that city's famous life-saving team. A long lens and a fast shutter speed enabled the photographer to reach out and stop the action. Special attention must be given to focusing in an action situation like this because when the subject is moving directly towards or away from the camera, the point of focus is constantly changing. "My early high school training as a photographer included covering sports, which forced me to compose quickly and to choose the most interesting moment from a sequence."

NIKON F W/MOTOR-DRIVE
105mm f2.5 NIKKOR
KODACHROME II
1/8 SEC. AT f4

Edgeworth was given an assignment by Esquire magazine to do a series of portraits of young British officers. He employed window light in much the same way the 17th-century Dutch painters did for their formal portraits. The medium telephoto lens is ideal for portraiture because it's long enough to eliminate unwanted distortion, yet permits the photographer to remain close enough to the subject to direct the poses in a normal conversational tone, thus making it easier to establish a rapport.

NIKON F W/MOTOR-DRIVE
200mm f4 NIKKOR
KODACHROME II
1/125 SEC. AT f5.6

This shot is part of a story Edgeworth produced on grouse hunting in Scotland. Edgeworth used a long lens to isolate the hunters and their dogs against the late afternoon sky. He took advantage of the subtle beauty of the gathering mauve clouds by shooting from a low angle and composing his picture so that the clouds would take up most of the frame.

NIKON F
105MM f2.5 NIKKOR
KODACHROME II
1/125 SEC. AT f5.6

Shooting out the window of his hotel in the village of Hawick, Edgeworth captured the particular quality of the Scottish winter light as it played on the walls and windows of the buildings along this side street.

NIKON F
20mm f3.5 NIKKOR
KODACHROME II
POLARIZING FILTER
1/30 SEC. AT f16

Edgeworth was hired by a South American airline to do a series of posters of Brazil. Here, he's captured the futuristic quality of the architecture of the capital, Brasilia, by framing the white buildings against the sky and darkening it with a polarizing filter. "I used an ultra-wide-angle lens to exaggerate the shapes and perspective." In addition to darkening the sky, a polarizing filter can be used to reduce or completely eliminate reflections in water, on leaves or on other shiny non-metallic objects.

NIKON F2
20mm f3.5 NIKKOR
INFRARED FILM
RED FILTER
EXPOSURE NOT RECORDED

The photographer's brother was the model for this modern-day crucifixion image taken on the main highway leading into Taos, New Mexico. The photograph was made on infrared film to help create a spiritual effect. "We had to work fast because cars kept coming along the road doing about 80 miles an hour."

NIKON F2
20mm f3.5 NIKKOR
KODACHROME II
POLARIZING FILTER
1/30 SEC. AT f22

The subject is a tiny church on an Indian reservation near Taos, New Mexico. "The interior is only large enough to accommodate 5 or 6 peo-

ple at a time. The only way I could get all of the crosses into the frame was to lie on my back just outside the gate and shoot up with a 20mm lens." Funk copied the original Kodachrome slide on Ektachrome X, rated at ASA 64, which he had processed as a negative so that the colors would revert to their complements. He used a polarizing filter to produce a dark sky in the original because he wanted a light sky in the final transparency. That's not as confusing as it sounds. Since the final transparency is actually a color negative, everything comes out the opposite of the tones in the original scene.

NIKON FTN
500mm f8 REFLEX NIKKOR
KODACHROME II
1/8 SEC. AT f8 (STATUE)
1/30 SEC. AT f8 (CHILDREN)

"For some time I had wanted to do a picture using one of the statues that you find all over Central Park. First I shot up into the face of the statue, using my hand to blur the edges of the picture. Then I rewound the film and photographed the two children on the same frame." The late af-

ternoon sun was low and facing into the lens for the second exposure and Funk again used his hand in front of the lens. This time the strong backlight caused his skin to act as a filter, turning the light to a golden orange.

NIKON FTN
200mm f4 NIKKOR (DAM AND SUN)
20mm f3.5 NIKKOR (WARNING LIGHT)
KODACHROME II
DEEP BLUE FILTER
EXPOSURES NOT RECORDED

This striking study in color contrast was done by exposing three separate images on a single transparency. Funk began by photographing the boy walking on the dam and then, just a few minutes later, recorded the setting sun. A special filter, originally intended for creating the "day for night" effect in motion pictures, was used to achieve the deep, overall blue. The final image, a red warning light, was added more than a week later. When working with multiple exposures, Funk remembers the precise shape and placement of each subject on each frame without the aid of notes or sketches, even though days or weeks may elapse between exposures.

NIKON F2
135mm f2.8 NIKKOR
KODACHROME II
1/60 SEC. AT f5.6

This picture of Notre Dame is part of a huge series Hidalgo is doing on the city of Paris, his adopted home. The blurred, romantic effect was obtained by putting a special grating screen in front of the lens. Hidalgo finds that the pictures he does for his own pleasure are the ones that appear in print most often.

NIKON F2
500mm f8 REFLEX NIKKOR
80-200mm ZOOM NIKKOR
KODACHROME II
EXPOSURES NOT RECORDED

Hidalgo did this study of a Japanese Buddha while on assignment for Air France.

The picture consists of four separate exposures on a single frame. Using a piece of black cardboard to block the right-hand side of the frame, Hidalgo recorded the close-up of the Buddha's face with his 500mm. The center picture was done in the same manner, this time using two image-repeater lenses in front of his zoom lens. The Buddha in the top right-hand corner was taken with the zoom at the 135mm setting and the two overlapping Buddhas below were done with a single image-repeater lens in front of the zoom set at 200mm. All exposures were done from exactly the same spot.

NIKON F2
50mm f1.4 NIKKOR
HIGH SPEED EKTACHROME
1/30 SEC. AT f2

The scene is a cafe during Carnival time in Zurich, Switzerland. Hidalgo turned it into something out of a Fellini movie by using a special attachment in front of his lens that creates a ghost-like image around everything in the picture. The effect is strongest with the lens at its widest opening.

NIKON F
400mm f4.5 NIKKOR
KODACHROME II
1/60 SEC. AT f4.5

"This was taken right after a heavy rain, when the atmosphere was completely clear. It is a single exposure and not, like many people think, a sandwich or double exposure." Hidalgo used a long telephoto lens to create the illusion of the elevator train being immediately next to the Eiffel Tower. In reality, they are a good distance apart.

NIKON F
24mm f2.8 NIKKOR
KODACHROME II
EXPOSURE NOT RECORDED

"I have an affinity for empty rooms and empty apartments. There's something mysterious about a place where people once lived but no longer do." Kane isolated the model's long legs in this unusual fashion illustration.

NIKON F
24mm f2.8 NIKKOR
KODACHROME II
EXPOSURE NOT RECORDED

This photograph was originally done as part of a group of illustrations of Bob Dylan songs. The subtle highlight flare was added to the picture by the photographer first touching his finger to the side of his nose and then to just the right spot on the lens. The natural oil caused the bright area to glow and spread into the surrounding shadows. A more intense version of this effect can be produced by smearing petroleum jelly on a clear filter.

NIKON F
24mm f2.8 NIKKOR
KODACHROME II
EXPOSURE NOT RECORDED

For this illustration of a modern-day Eve, Kane again chose an empty room as the location. This time the barren apartment was his own "... just before the furniture arrived." Kane is particularly fond of the quality of light that is produced in such an environment.

NIKON F
24mm f2.8 NIKKOR
KODACHROME II
EXPOSURE NOT RECORDED

Kane intentionally underexposed this transparency, taken late one afternoon on a deserted beach in the Caribbean, so that only the figure of the woman and the sweeping lines of the sand would remain visble. The 24mm Nikkor has been Kane's favorite wide-angle for the last few years because of its intrinsic lack of distortion. "Photographers, like all artists, go through different periods. Presently, I'm not using my wide-angles much. I'm shooting mostly with the normal 50mm and the 55mm lenses." Kane caused a sensation in the photography world when he chose an ultra-wide-angle lens to photograph women's fashions in the early 1960s.

NIKON F W/MOTOR-DRIVE
180mm f2.8 NIKKOR
KODACHROME II
1/250 SEC. AT f2.8

Kirkland held his motorized camera just above the water's surface at the edge of a pool in Miami, Florida, and focused through the Nikon right-angle viewing attachment. This special finder permits viewing from any angle 90° off the camera's optical axis. The photographer's assistant used a palm leaf to shade the model's face.

NIKON F
105mm f2.5 NIKKOR
KODACHROME X
1/500 SEC. AT f2.8

Kirkland recorded the flight of this ancient biplane while doing publicity photography for the film 'The Magnificent Men in Their Flying Machines' The photographer arranged

to have the door of the helicopter removed and himself strapped into place half in and half out of the hatchway. "I was outfitted with earphones and a mike so that I could talk with the copter pilot over the sound of the engine and tell him where I wanted to be in relation to the antique aircraft." Kirkland recommends using a shutter speed of 1/250 second or faster for this kind of shooting in order to compensate for the vibrations of the helicopter. The late afternoon light, not a special filter, was responsible for the picture's extraordinary golden brown cast.

NIKON F
180mm f2.8 NIKKOR
KODACHROME II
1/60 SEC. AT f4

Although this picture has a candid, grab-shot quality about it, it was in fact entirely planned. The children were hired from a Tokyo model agency and the sign was specially commissioned by Kirkland. The Japanese symbol stands for "east" or "Orient" and the photo was done for the cover of a spe-

cial issue of Look magazine on that part of the world. "As a matter of fact, the paint on the sign was still wet when we did the picture. The sign painter was late finishing it and we had to set things up on the street right outside his shop in order to make our tight deadline."

NIKON F W/MOTOR-DRIVE
20mm f3.5 NIKKOR
KODACHROME II
1/2 SEC. AT f22

Kirkland used himself and his wife Francoise as models in this photograph taken to illustrate an article about America's "back to the land" movement. The camera's cordless battery and motor functioned as a camera stand and Kirkland fired the shutter by using a radio device which was held out of sight in his left hand. Here again, the photographer made use of the Nikon right-angle viewfinder.

NIKON F
20mm f3.5 NIKKOR
KODACHROME II
2 SEC. AT f5.6

Lawlor taped a purple-tinted sunglass lens in front of his wide-angle and bracketed a number of long exposures so that the water would be totally blurred. "I have several of these tinted filters. This one is colored on the top and clear on the bottom, with the areas fading into one another. The ones you buy in any eyeglass shop seem to work best, but they need to be large enough to be taped to the front of the lens without causing vignetting."

NIKON F2 W/MOTOR-DRIVE
80-200mm NIKKOR ZOOM
KODACHROME II
1/125 SEC. AT f4.5

This striking portrait was taken in a pit stop in Monte Carlo during the Grand Prix. "There is a great deal of frantic activity in the pits. The zoom gives maximum flexibility under this kind of cramped conditions."

NIKON F2 W/MOTOR-DRIVE
500mm f8 REFLEX NIKKOR
KODACHROME X
1/500 SEC. AT f8

Lawlor was waiting for the stock car races to begin at Watkins Glen when he looked up and saw this parachutist floating across the sky with a smoke bomb attached to his leg. "I literally pulled the camera out of the hands of my assistant and was able to squeeze off three shots before it was over."

NIKON F
20mm f3.5 NIKKOR
KODACHROME II
POLARIZING FILTER
1/250 SEC. AT f8

The photographer had been traveling in Malaysia for several weeks doing figure photography for a British calendar company. This graphic semi-still life was done strictly for himself, as a creative change of pace. "Working this close with an extreme wide-angle, I had to be careful to keep all the parts of the subject on the same plane, at an equal distance from the camera; otherwise, I'd have ended up with a lot of distortion."

NIKON F
28mm f3.5 NIKKOR
KODACHROME II
85 FILTER
EXPOSURE NOT RECORDED

"I had already been in this Peruvian mountain village for several days and people had become used to me taking pictures of them." Lawlor used an orange filter to counteract the blue ultra-violet effect one sometimes comes across at altitudes above 10,000 feet. In this instance, the filter also served to cut down the contrast.

NIKON F W/MOTOR-DRIVE
180mm f2.8 NIKKOR
KODACHROME II
1/125 SEC. AT f4

The snake charmer was going through his act in the Bazaar in Marrakesh, Morocco when Maisel captured both him and his reptile friend on film. The 180mm's f/2.8 opening permits handholding in low light with reasonably fast shutter speeds. Most prolific photographers agree that every focal length has its own particular optical personality. To Maisel, the 180mm is an old friend.

NIKON F W/MOTOR-DRIVE
50mm f1.4 NIKKOR
KODACHROME II
1/125 SEC. AT f4

The afternoon light coming through the bathroom window served to accent the lines of the female figure. "I would like to do more on the erotic theme. This is a very basic, important area of life that has rarely been handled well by photographers."

NIKON F W/MOTOR-DRIVE
500mm f8 REFLEX NIKKOR
KODACHROME II
UV FILTER
1/125 SEC. AT f8

Maisel recorded this dramatic sunrise from the roof of his building in lower Manhattan. A tripod was used here but whenever possible Maisel prefers to hand-hold his long lenses. He feels that by shooting this way he can remain loose and flexible and ready to take advantage of the nuances of a changing situation. He now prefers the P screen for use with his long lenses. "You have to keep your elbows in close to your body, control your breathing, brace yourself against something sturdy like a wall, the way you would with a rifle."

NIKON F
180mm f2.8 NIKKOR
KODACHROME II
1/125 SEC. AT f5.6

The light itself is really the subject of this photograph of the sunset reflected in the windows of an office building in lower Manhattan. Maisel prefers to shoot color either in the morning or very late in the afternoon when the sun is low and dramatic and the light is most interesting.

NIKON F W/MOTOR-DRIVE
180mm f2.8 NIKKOR
KODACHROME II
1/250 SEC. AT f5.6

By using a telephoto lens, Maisel was able to frame the picture the way he wanted it without moving in too close to the bird and perhaps frightening it away. This picture was part of a series Maisel did for a book on the oil-rich country of Iran.

NIKON FTN
200mm f4 NIKKOR
INFRARED FILM
GREEN FILTER (CHURCH)
1/250 SEC. AT f5.6 (CHURCH)
1/250 SEC. AT f11 (WATER)

McCarthy wanted to convey the special fantasy quality of the Italian city of Venice. He used infrared color film with a green filter on his telephoto lens to record the dome of St. Mark's Cathedral, then removed the filter and rewound the frame to add the image of the water in the Grand Canal.

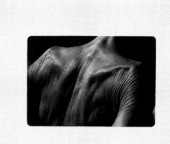

NIKON F
300mm f4.5 NIKKOR
KODACHROME II
1/250 SEC. AT f11

McCarthy used a long lens with the M-ring, a closeup tube designed for use with the 55mm f/3.5 Auto Micro Nikkor. When used in con-

junction with a telephoto, the M-ring permits the photographer to focus the lens in tight for closeups such as this one. "With a really long lens, the people often think that I'm shooting something way off in the distance beyond them when all the time I'm really doing closeups of a person standing just a few feet away." McCarthy feels that people never really know that you've snapped their picture until you advance the film with your thumb. "That's the giveaway. I turn my back and walk a few feet before I wind."

NIKON F
105mm f2.5 NIKKOR
KODACHROME II
DARK RED FILTER
1/1000 SEC. AT f22

This picture was originally taken to illustrate the "Wings of Man" theme of Eastern Airlines. McCarthy arranged the shooting for early morning so that the sun would be at a convenient angle, just above the horizon. "Shooting directly into the sun calls for a very brief exposure even with a deep red filter." The setting was a hotel swimming pool in Miami Beach, Florida. The diving board is just out of sight, below the frame.

NIKON F
20mm f3.5 NIKKOR
TRI-X FOR ORIGINAL
1/250 SEC. AT f22

The original picture of this Brooklyn child was taken on black-and-white film. Then McCarthy made a 16 x 20" black-and-white Kodalith transparency. Placing the Kodalith face down on his light box, McCarthy proceeded to hand-color the emulsion side of the enlarged black-and-white transparency. When this was completed to his satisfaction, he made a copy of the hand-painted Kodalith on Kodachrome. The final result won the grand prize in a Life magazine photo contest.

NIKON F
400mm f4.5 NIKKOR
HIGH SPEED EKTACHROME
ORANGE FILTER
EXPOSURE NOT RECORDED

"The boat pulled up to just the right spot, between me and the sun, and I heard the coxswain call for a 15-second rest. I was able to get off four exposures before they moved on." Meola then wound the film back four frames and added the sun to the bottom of the picture, creating a giant orange exclamation mark under the boat. The film was processed as a negative in C-22 developer. In order to get a slide that had the same colors as the original scene, Meola duped the HSE color negative on Ektachrome-X and again processed the film as a negative.

NIKON F2 W/MOTOR-DRIVE
28mm f2 NIKKOR
KODACHROME II
1/15 SEC. AT f2

Meola scheduled his shooting for late in the afternoon so that the entire pool would be in deep shade. "I was kneeling on the edge of the pool, hand-holding the camera with both arms pressed against my sides because of the slow shutter speed. The hotel was not really open yet so there were very few people around." Meola duped the slide in order to add contrast to a rather flat original.

NIKON F2 W/MOTOR-DRIVE
80-200mm NIKKOR ZOOM
KODACHROME II
1/250 SEC. AT f5.6

Meola chose the zoom lens so that he could frame the sign exactly the way he wanted it from a fixed point across the street. "Almost as soon as I set up the shot, this boy came by who looked just right for the situation. Everyone else was dressed in brightly colored clothing but the boy had on nothing except white shorts that went perfectly with the red in the sign. I tried to get him to walk by several times but he was very timid and ran off after just one pass. I managed to

get 5 frames with one burst of the motor. The other 4 were disasters but happily this one worked." When Meola plans in advance to make a dupe of the original slide for one reason or another — here the reds in the sign were not as bright as he wanted them and he knew that duping would make them brighter — he leaves a little extra space in framing so that he can crop in slightly when making the copy. The dupe was made on Kodachrome II with a CC10 red filter.

NIKON F2 W/MOTOR-DRIVE
55mm AUTO MICRO-NIKKOR f3.5
KODACHROME II
1/4 SEC. AT f32

Meola happened upon this wall just outside of Port-au-Prince, Haiti. "The bricks were painted a bright, glossy red but the mortar between the bricks was white. I realized that by panning the camera from one side to the other I would get red and white stripes. Since the man passing had vertical stripes on his caftan, I decided to try to play one set of stripes against the other." Placing his camera on a tripod, Meola shot two rolls of color, varying the exposure between 1/15 and 1/4 second.

NIKON F
80-200mm NIKKOR ZOOM
KODACHROME II
1 SEC. AT f16

Obremski shot four separate frames of this Copenhagen Royal Palace Guard, zooming during each exposure. "I started by framing each shot at the widest end of the zoom and quickly zooming in all the way during the last part of the full second exposure. I deliberately overexposed each frame so that all four could later be sandwiched together and copied." Normal exposure, in this case, would have resulted in too dark a final image.

NIKON F2 W/MOTOR-DRIVE
28mm f3.5 NIKKOR
KODACHROME II
#3 NEUTRAL DENSITY FILTER
1/125 SEC. AT f11, 8 TIMES

"I wanted the building to be recognizable as Notre Dame so I used only eight exposures. If I had used a great many exposures on this shot, say 32 or 64, as I've done with some subjects, the image would have become too soft and I would have lost most of the Cathedral's identity." Obremski hand-holds most of his multiple exposures so that the images line up approximately rather than exactly. "I do this in order to achieve a very soft, impressionistic effect." When making multiple exposures on a single frame, it is necessary to close down one f-stop for each doubled exposure. Or, as Obremski did here, you may use a neutral density filter to effectively cut the exposure.

NIKON F2 W/MOTOR-DRIVE
28mm f3.5 NIKKOR
KODACHROME II
1/60 AT f16, 32 TIMES

Obremski wanted to do something with the line of gondolas and the motion of the water in Venice's Grand Canal. "The boats were bobbing up and down so I held my motorized Nikon F2 in one place and made a 32-exposure multiple by keeping my finger on the clutch button while firing."

NIKON F2 W/MOTOR-DRIVE
28mm f3.5 NIKKOR
KODACHROME II
1/125 SEC. AT f22, 8 TIMES

Obremski noticed that all the buildings facing onto this Amsterdam canal had similar facades. So he walked along the edge of the canal from one bridge to the next shooting eight separate but similar images one upon the other. "I try to anchor the image at one point in the frame, but I don't want an exact alignment of images, rather the opposite. I want them to overlap a bit."

NIKON F2
135mm f2.8 NIKKOR
KODACHROME II
1/125 SEC. AT f5.6

This is a straight shot of children playing in front of a fun-house mirror in Copenhagen's Tivoli Gardens. Here Obremski used a long lens to frame in close and not show the edge of the mirror. "I didn't want the fact that it was a reflection to be immediately apparent to the viewer. This would have ruined the fantasy feeling of the picture."

NIKON F2 W/MOTOR-DRIVE
28mm f3.5 NIKKOR
KODACHROME II
1/125 SEC. AT f11, TWICE

Covering the bottom half of his lens with a sheet of black paper, Obremski composed his picture in the unmasked area of the viewfinder and made his first exposure. After pressing the double exposure button and cocking the shutter without advancing the film, he turned the camera upside down and masked the section of the viewfinder that had been left clear the first time. Framing the subject again, in the same way, he made a second exposure. In each case, the black paper masked the half of the lens nearest the ground. "I was interested in the double reflection, the actual reflection in the water plus the fabricated reflection effect of the double image." This masking technique is by no means foolproof. You may end up with a thin black line in the center of the frame or an overlapping of the images where they come together. Placing two marks on the lens hood as a point of reference will help the photographer line up the mask correctly but even this is not 100 per cent accurate.

NIKON F2
55mm f3.5 AUTO MICRO-NIKKOR
KODACHROME TYPE A
EXPOSURE NOT RECORDED

Sarapochiello took advantage of the special double-exposure button on his F2 in order to combine these two closeups on one frame. When exact placement of the images is important, Sarapochiello sketches both images on a larger, scaled duplicate of the frame he sees in his F2 viewfinder.

NIKON F2
55mm f3.5 AUTO MICRO-NIKKOR
KODACHROME TYPE A
EXPOSURE NOT RECORDED

The eye belongs to a tiny Mexican 'santo' that the photographer brought back from a holiday trip a few years ago. The rope was bought at an odd-lot store in lower Manhattan. Sarapochiello favors working with a single light source and prefers that source to be photo flood rather than flash so that he can see exactly what he is getting.

NIKON F2
28mm f2 NIKKOR
HIGH SPEED EKTACHROME TYPE B
EXPOSURE NOT RECORDED

Sarapochiello came upon this weather-beaten child's sandal on a Long Island beach. "I had to bring it back to the studio to do the picture. On the real beach there were a lot of other things lying around — pieces of wood, shells, candy wrappers. Everything was in the way. On my beach there's nothing but the sandal." A single 3200K flood was the only light.

NIKON F2
135mm f2.8 NIKKOR
KODACHROME TYPE A
EXPOSURE NOT RECORDED

The mask-like object is made of wood and was found in the street near Sarapochiello's New York studio. "It probably fell off the front of one of the old houses in the neighborhood. The holes were already in it so I bought some glass eyes from a taxidermy shop and put together this creature." The photographer used a No. 1 closeup lens in front of his telephoto so that he could move in tight.

NIKON F2 W/MOTOR-DRIVE
35mm f1.4 NIKKOR (DIVER)
500mm f8 REFLEX NIKKOR (SUN)
KODACHROME II
EXPOSURES NOT RECORDED

In planning this picture, Steedman decided that he wanted the late afternoon sun to be right behind the diver. "This does happen but not at that particular time of the year. I needed to have a completely clear sky for the sandwich so I deliberately overexposed about 2 stops. That way, I was able to retain a semi-silhouette effect on the diver and at the same time bring out some detail in the rocks." Steedman has a large stock of pictures of the sun in different positions that he uses for sandwiches and double printing. "From time to time I go out on a hazy day and shoot the sun with a variety of lenses, bracketing the exposures, so that I'll have everything from a washed-out pale disk to a dark orange ball."

NIKON FTN
85mm f1.8 NIKKOR
KODACHROME II
1/125 SEC. AT f2

Steedman was taking a coffee break from an advertising assignment on Nantucket Island off the coast of New England when he noticed this local resident in a private moment. The photographer used a medium telephoto lens from across the room so as not to intrude on the woman or shatter her mood.

NIKON FTN
24mm f2.8 NIKKOR
EKTACHROME-X
1/125 SEC. AT f2.8

"The boy had been watching me take pictures of a monument near Spanish Town, Jamaica. I don't know why he had such a serious, heavy look on his face." Steedman moved in close with a wide-angle and built his composition around the

contrasting lines of the fence and the boy's arms.

NIKON F2
20mm f3.5 NIKKOR (MOUNTAINS)
500mm f8 MIRROR LENS (MOON)
KODACHROME II
POLARIZING FILTER (MOUNTAINS)
EXPOSURES NOT RECORDED

Steedman stopped down his wide-angle lens all the way to f/22 in order to retain the dramatic sculptured effect that was caused by the setting sun hitting the mountains at an angle. He used a polarizing filter to darken the sky and bring out maximum detail in the sand and rock. The moon was added in the darkroom by double printing the two images onto Kodak 6120 duping film. "The moon must be underexposed to bring out the valleys; otherwise, you'll end up with nothing but a white circle." Steedman had to make a Kodalith mask for the transparency of the moon because he had shot the original from a rooftop in New York City and it turned out that a great deal of ambient light had been present, which turned the sky a dull gray. Double printing works best when additional images can be printed onto a completely black area.

NIKON F
55mm f3.5 AUTO MICRO-NIKKOR
KODACHROME II
1/30 SEC. AT f5.6

Turner produced this unusual closeup of a Masai warrior's ear while doing an essay on East Africa for Esquire. "The Masai people in this region feel the ear to be a sacred part of the body and in order to enforce this belief they attach all kinds of objects to it such as tin cans, cork, film canisters and safety pins." Turner chose soft, natural north light in order to bring out detail in both the shadows and highlights.

NIKON F
20mm f3.5 NIKKOR
KODACHROME TYPE A
CC100B FILTER
5 MINUTES AT f3.5

Turner was asked by a South American airline to try to come up with a picture that would convey the uniqueness of the famous Salt Cathedral located hundreds of feet below the surface of the earth in a salt mine about an hour's drive from the city of Bogota, Colombia. Turner requested that thirty or forty nuns be brought to the underground church from a nearby convent. The nuns were posed at intervals throughout the church interior. With a custom-made CC100 blue filter in front of his lens, Turner bracketed the exposures, which ran 4 to 6 minutes with the lens wide open. "I used both Type A film and the strong filter because very long exposures tend to go warm and I wanted the picture to be blue and cool in order to get across the feeling of being underground." Turner said his greatest problem was keeping the nuns from moving during the long exposures.

NIKON F
20mm f3.5 NIKKOR
KODACHROME II
1/2 SEC. AT f3.5

Focusing on the futuristic lines of the Hyatt Regency Hotel in Houston, Texas, Turner deliberately mismatched his film

and light source to create this exciting graphic. Any material that is intended for use in daylight goes warm and shows a strong, overall orange-red hue when used with tungsten light.

NIKON F
20mm f3.5 NIKKOR
KODACHROME TYPE A
CCB50 FILTER
1/15 SEC. AT f3.5

Entering an eerie world of billowing smoke and showering hot ash, Turner documented the fury of an erupting volcano as it buried the city of Vestmannaeyjar on the Icelandic island of Heimaey. Turner used a blue filter and Type A indoor film to enhance the cool shades of dawn and to provide a complement to the strong reds and yellows of the volcano's fiery eruption. Type A film is designed to deal with the strong, intrinsic reds of incandescent light. Therefore, the film shows an overall blue tint when used in natural light.

NIKON FTN
20mm f3.5 NIKKOR
KODACHROME II
SKYLIGHT FILTER
1/60 SEC. AT f11

Walking along an Eastern Long Island beach after a storm, Wolf came across a dead shark that had been washed up onto the sand. Using a wide-angle lens, the photographer framed his picture so that the straight lines of the horizon would serve as a contrast to the soft, sweeping lines of the fish. Wolf's training as a designer is evident in his precise yet delicate compositions.

NIKON F2
55mm f3.5 AUTO MICRO-NIKKOR
KODACHROME II
SKYLIGHT FILTER
1/30 SEC. AT f11

In Florence, Italy, Wolf came upon this reflection in the window of a small shop. He was fascinated by the reflection's three-dimensional

quality, created by the open door to the street at the far end of the room. Wolf stopped the lens down as much as he could in order to increase his depth of field and achieve an overall sharpness in all three images.

NIKON FTN
135mm f2.8 NIKKOR
KODACHROME II
SKYLIGHT FILTER
1/60 SEC. AT f4.5

Wolf had been working with the model for some time trying to come up with a picture that would best illustrate a new shade of lipstick by Elizabeth Arden. "The girl asked me if she could eat one of the mangos and suddenly there was the picture I wanted." With strongly back-lit subjects such as this one, the exposure should be arrived at by taking a reading in the shadow area and then underexposing 1 or 2 stops.

NIKON F
50mm f1.4 NIKKOR
KODACHROME II
SKYLIGHT FILTER
1/125 SEC. AT f8

"You find these signs all over the snow trails in Switzerland. They warn the skier of a sudden sharp drop on the other side of the hill." Wolf used the shape and the color of the sign as a design element with a comic touch in an otherwise stark, empty landscape. It's usually a good idea to underexpose slightly when taking pictures of snow in order to retain detail in the overall white area.

NIKON F2
55mm f3.5 AUTO MICRO-NIKKOR
KODACHROME II
1/60 SEC. AT f8

Designer Milton Glaser asked Wolf to come up with a personal idea for a Valentine card for an issue of Audience magazine. Wolf used an electronic flash bounced off an umbrella to one side of the model. When light is bounced off a broad surface, such as an umbrella, it has a softer, less contrasty quality and gives more detail in the shadow areas.

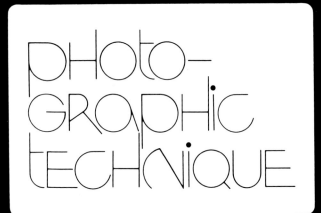

PHOTO-GRAPHIC TECHNIQUE

If you're like many of us, you'll look at the marvelous collection of images in this book... and be inspired to go out and create your own. You can! But many of our 17 photographers have employed some fairly sophisticated principles and techniques. So, to help you in your personal quest for great photographs, we have prepared this special educational section. It includes details on five especially useful subjects—which also relate directly to the photographs in this book.

composition

Mastering the mechanical operations of a camera and its accessories is a relatively simple matter. There are certain operations which must be understood and can be mastered with a reasonable amount of practice. To understand and master the control of esthetic qualities, that is the subject matter in your photographs, is much more difficult. It involves the art of recognizing a potential photograph, which can be developed readily enough, with training and intuition, but it involves the photographer with elements that are, by and large, uncontrollable. It is well nigh impossible, for instance, to move a tree from one side of a meadow to another in order to improve the arrangement of the parts of a picture you want to take. With the exception of the photojournalist, who must take his subjects as they come, and of the studio photographer, who can arrange his subject matter to his heart's content, the composition of a photograph is possibly the most challenging aspect of the entire craft of photography.

Fortunately the 35mm slr camera has been designed with the human being in mind. We are all accustomed to looking at the world from our own individual height and this camera allows us to photograph it from eye level. Our perception is basically a horizontal view and the camera is oriented this way. However, should we decide to narrow our vision and direct it upward, the 35mm camera is easily adaptable to vertical use. The rectangular format of the 35mm negative is psychologically in tune with our seeing habits. If one can generalize about such subjective

matters, horizontal scenes such as landscapes are restful, vertical scenes are more active and dynamic.

Short of being able to move that tree, there are some basic rules of composition that can be learned and mastered, either after or concurrently with the mastering of your equipment. The essential factor in the procedure is to get to know your lenses and what they can do, what each is particularly suited for. For instance, the medium telephoto lens — 85 to 135mm — has long been considered the ideal lens for portraits. It allows you to take pictures in which the subject's head fills the entire frame without distortion of the features usually accompanied by close focusing with shorter focal length lenses. This is accomplished from a shooting distance of less than 10 feet, which enables the photographer to be both close enough to the subject to carry on conversation when necessary and far enough away when his presence might become distracting.

Aside from the perspective achieved with short (normal and wide-angle) lenses, there are a few other basic inherent characteristics to consider. Wide-angle lenses naturally spread out the subject matter of scenic shots when taken at "normal" shooting distances and compress it in size to produce a generous foreground and background area. Telephoto lenses, on the other hand, enlarge the central portion of a scene and compress the entire area so that the foreground and background tend to blend into one another.

Finally, there is the matter of depth-of-field, the area of ac-

ceptably sharp focus. With c lenses, the smaller the apertur the greater the depth-of-field Using the same aperture on v ious focal length lenses at th same subject distance, the shorter focal length lenses pr duce a greater depth of sha focus. And with all lenses, foct ing to infinity, results in great depth-of-field.

This information becomes useful in a situation such as th you wish to take a portrait o someone in an outdoor settir — a field of green grass, befo a stand of trees, etc. For a pleasing effect you can use long (105mm or more) lens at wide aperture. This allows yo to fill nearly the whole frame with the face while throwing th background out of focus. The result: the background becomes unobtrusive and com pliments, rather than dominat the face. This is precisely the technique followed by Morto Beebe in his portrait of the young Polynesian girl, page

Perhaps the best way to lea the capabilities of the variou lenses is with a zoom lens. Merely putting it on camera and observing its effects on th subject — area, image size, depth-of-field — will give you good idea of what happens t various subjects at various dis tances and apertures with th different focal length lenses.

An essential rule in compos tion, as in many other actions, i to keep it simple. You should t to fill the frame as much as pos sible with just the essential suk ject. This can be done either by changing your shooting distance (moving in closer) o using a longer focal length len Of course, with a zoom lens th selective "cropping" within th camera is relatively easy. Kee e background simple. Make a part of the picture rather an a distracting element. cusing and depth-of-field, as tlined in the example above, an also be controlled so that e principal subject area receives the most emphasis, and e background becomes an distinct mass that sets the ain subject apart. If you can ontrol your main subject, ace it within a large, plain ea of contrasting color, texre and tone.

Avoid cutting off large apes at the edges of your ame, as this tends to lead the ewer's eye out of the picture. is is not to say that the essenal part of the subject should ways be in the exact center of e picture, but the eye should ways be directed into, rather an out of, the picture. Lines, ch as the converging parallel es of a building or railroad cks or the furrows of a owed field, should always ad the eye to the main point interest. The snake in Jay aisel's view of a Moroccan harmer on page 56 is not this pe of line, in the strictest sense the word, but it does serve to

lead the eye precisely in the direction Maisel wants.

If you must end up with a large area of no particular interest, it is better to sacrifice the background and retain the essential elements in the foreground. You can avoid the pitfalls of either too much foreground or too much background by including an object close to the camera in an upper or lower corner of your picture frame. This object, frequently an overhanging branch or bit of shrubbery or rock, provides a natural framework to the scene as well as helping fill the void caused by the large, undetailed area.

Another side of this same coin, primarily in scenic shots, is to place the main area of in-

terest slightly below the horizontal midpoint as Beebe has done with the New Guinea fisherman on page 2. This exceptional photographic study, which opens this volume, also illustrates another rule of good composition. We mentioned earlier that vertical pictures generally suggest action and movement. Motion is also best expressed in subjects that

move, or direct the eye, along diagonal lines from one upper corner to the opposite lower corner. This is precisely the direction in which the native boatman is traveling.

One theory of good composition suggests the dividing of the picture area into three equal parts, both horizontally and vertically, and then placing the principal and secondary subjects at the various points of intersection of these areas. Thus the main area of interest would never be in the center of the picture area. (This theory is obviously somewhat akin to the rules mentioned above regarding elimination of wasted foreground space and the below-the-midline placement.) A graphic example of this grid-like pattern placement is evident in the scene on pages 59 and 60 by Maisel in which the bird is slightly off center and, by pure coincidence, at the intersection of horizontal and vertical lines roughly corresponding to the three-part divisions.

Somewhat less precise mathematically are the desirable shapes and configurations found in nature that rep-

resent sought after subject matter. Probably the best known in this group is the "S" curve. This pleasing and interesting phenomenon appears frequently throughout this volume, most notably on pages 41 and

42 in Art Kane's beach scene and Henry Wolf's similar effort on page 98. But, as in all matters esthetic, neither picture follows the rules to the letter and does not present the classic S curve. Kane's is a partial S which is merely one element in an overall design pattern, while Wolf's dead shark is the chief point of interest that must still be

augmented by another contrasting element, namely the straight horizontal line of water in the far background. Such contrasting elements, whether of shapes, mass, tone or hue, are also desirable factors in good composition.

In addition to contrast, balance of various elements aids the final pictorial result. Thus Maisel's three windows on page 58 represent various intensities of light with the brightest and most intense flanked by equally attracting, though differing in intensity, shapes of equal size and shape. The photograph immediately above the three windows shows Maisel's use of elements of contrasting shapes. The straight-lined, rectangular buildings lead the eye upward to the round, not yet fully formed rising

sun. Mitchell Funk employs similar shapes (pages 29 and 30) of varying sizes in a multiple exposure that expresses balance as well as movement in the classic, diagonal direction despite the fact that here the movement is directed upwards from the large to the small circular shape. Again, for contrast and interest, a horizontal shape has been added.

Good composition technique applies equally to black-and-white photography as to color. In the former, arrangement of the subject elements is more difficult because the tonal differences exist only in brightness and contrast. In color there are many more variables including, among others, the colors themselves plus variations in hue, tone, saturation, luminosity, and temperature (red tones represent warmth; blue tones, coolness). Color gives the photographer much more to work with but also creates potentially more pitfalls.

In addition to the rules listed earlier there are a few others designed to aid color photography specifically. Once again simplicity is of prime importance. Try to include a few large single-colored masses rather than the entire spectrum of smaller, multi-colored objects. Avoid clashing of colors that are not pleasing to the eye. Cool colors are best for backgrounds while the warmer hues work best in foregrounds. Highly saturated colors, such as the two bright circles in Funk's work, serve as a spotlight to place the emphasis on a desired object. The out-of-focus background, as previously pointed out, often better serves the total picture than a clearly defined one. And

finally, as we discuss in anoth chapter, the judicious use o colored filters can add immeasureably to the final res

Photography is an active and the best way to master it to pursue it constantly. The basic rules for composition given here are a good starti point. As you try to incorpora one or two into your picture: the desired effect will come more naturally. In seeking th diagonal movement, for example, you may chance up the complete or partial S curn Indeed, you may end up wi both. It is apparent, by now, that many of the pictures in book do, indeed, show exc lent examples of several ba compositional techniques us together harmoniously.

Then, of course, there are t exceptions that always mak the rules. In many cases, the exceptions improve upon th rules. Kane's S curve on the beach (pages 41-42) presen a vast foreground area. Far from destroying the total effe this mass provides a suitable stage on which the other tw elements — water and womc — can be properly positione Whether you will eventually wish to express yourself, pho graphically, by the rules or against them, it is a good ide to master them first and ther strike out in whichever directi your imagination takes you.

MULTIPLE EXPOSURE

There was a time, not long ago, when a double exposure was considered just about the worst mistake one could make in photography. Whether it was technical incompetence or just bad form has never really been determined, but it was a fate to be avoided at all costs. The earliest cameras—in fact most cameras built up until the mid 1930's — had separate film advance and shutter cocking mechanisms. Not only did this mean two distinct operations had to be performed by the photographer, it also opened the way for that unwanted action to occur and reoccur. By forgetting to wind the film after taking a picture, the photographer was susceptible to the unintentional superimposed set of images on one frame of film.

Most modern cameras, with the notable exception of the larger format press and view models, now have a combined wind and shutter cocking system, which was no doubt developed to save the camera operator an extra step. Since the two operations are interdependent it seemed logical to combine them. It also eliminated the specter of the double exposure — until the relatively recent past when the double exposure suddenly became an object of love if not entirely of art. Photographers began experimenting with the technique and it gradually attained its present stature as a highly artistic aspect of the medium.

It followed, then, that if one extra exposure could improve the esthetic quality of a photograph, perhaps several extra exposures would compound the improvement, and the multiple exposure became a reality. As partial proof we cite a few of the photographers represented in this volume who chose this technique in the making of the self portraits that appear at the start of the section devoted to their work: Mitchell Funk on page 25, George Obremski on page 73 and Pete Turner on page 91.

The growing popularity of multiple exposures stems from a two-fold need — to improve and/or correct existing pictures and to provide the photographer with a technique for carrying out more artistic means of expression. (In some ways, multiple exposure photography is akin to the slide sandwich technique which is covered in the chapter on Slide Copying.) Perhaps its most

MULTIPLE EXPOSURE

readily adaptable task is in creating abstract patterns and designs.

With some older cameras it is literally impossible to make an intentional double exposure, but most cameras today, still equipped with the "double exposure prevention" provision, may still be used to produce the double exposure with a minimum effort. The most direct path to intentional multiple exposures is to disengage the film advance operation from the shutter cocking operation. To accomplish this you must first tighten up the film in its cassette by turning the rewind crank in the rewinding direction without pressing the release button on the bottom of the camera, as you would normally do. This should be done gently and you should stop when the film first offers resistance to further winding. Next you must hold the crank tightly so that the film will remain stationary when you

wind the film advance-shutter cock lever. But before you operate the advance lever you must press in the release button on the bottom. In short, you may need three good working fingers: one to hold the rewind crank taut, one to keep the release button depressed in case it won't stay depressed and one to operate the shutter-cocking lever. What actually happens inside the camera is that the sprocket wheel that usually advances the film becomes disengaged while the shutter cocking proceeds in the normal fashion.

While assuring that the succeeding exposure, or exposures, will thus fall on the previously exposed negative, this method does not insure perfect registration and requires that the frame following the multiple exposure be left blank, since the next time you move the advance lever, complete film transport may not occur.

There's another method of making multiple exposures which may be easier, but it involves more memory work. After loading the film and just before closing the camera back, some photographers put a mark on the film leader opposite another mark on the camera (either their own mc

or some object in the camera itself, such as the sprocket wheel). Whenever they want double expose they rewind the roll of film almost completely back into its cassette, leaving the leader extended as it is when it comes out of the box. They must then reload the film carefully, aligning the marks insure that succeeding frames will fall precisely "on top" of the first set of exposures. Then it is just a matter of advancing the film until you reach the desired negative and taking the second exposure.

You must, of course, have some sort of record of which picture is on which frame so that you don't double expose the wrong one and, need we say if you must keep your lens cap on while clicking off the frames on your way to reaching the desired negative. This method, too, is not absolutely foolproof as the alignment of the marks may not be as precise as you wish. This is the technique used

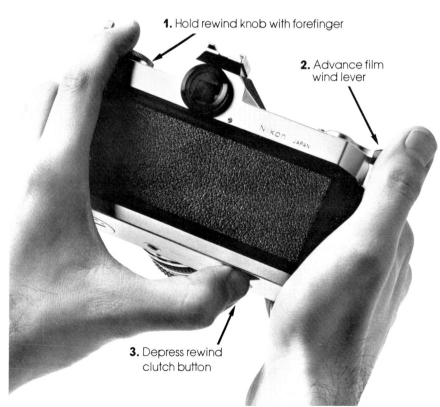

1. Hold rewind knob with forefinger

2. Advance film wind lever

3. Depress rewind clutch button

y Mitchell Funk, Pete Turner and many other masters of the multiple. They may wind off an entire roll (using a motor-driven camera) of one element of the multiple. Then they rewind and shoot the whole roll again on a second subject. The result is a whole set of variations on a theme from which to choose.

Closely related to multiple exposures is the technique of the split frame image in which several smaller pictures are made on one frame of film. A good example is the scene on page 78 by George Obremski. This method involves masking off part of the picture while retaining the frame in place as for a multiple exposure. He first shot his scene normally except for placing a piece of stiff black

paper over the bottom half of his lens. For his second exposure he turned the camera upside down, and masked off the bottom half again (the second bottom had become the first top, which had been previously exposed).

Obremski suggests using a lens shade and marking it so that you know where to place your masking paper. Even then, he says, the alignment may not be exact and you are liable to end up with a black line between the two mirror images or an area of overlapping at the point where the two images meet. In some cases, as with Turner's self portrait and its black background, you can turn this uncertainty to your advantage.

The involved methods of obtaining multiple exposures, described above, have prompted some camera manufacturers to incorporate a multiple exposure provision into their cameras. Today, on some of the top models, a simple button or lever disengages the wind mechanism from the shutter cocking, thus enabling you to superimpose exposures on top of one another to your heart's content. The Nikon F2 was the first 35mm slr camera to offer precise multiple exposure registration—the photographer need only depress the rewind clutch button and wind the film advance lever to prepare for the second exposure. George Obremski carried this capability to its ultimate for his multiple view of the Venetian gondolas (page 76) taken with his motorized F2. He simply held his finger on the release while advancing the film via the motor in short quick bursts (the motor drive has its own clutch button release). He deliberately hand

held the camera to produce slightly misaligned pictures and, therefore, the blurred effect (only possible on this camera).

Making multiple exposures involves another basic photographic action — exposure compensation. Since the final picture must adhere to the proper exposure setting indicated by the meter, its various parts (the multiple exposures) must add up to that predetermined setting. In other words, for a double exposure you should give each "take" one half the exposure it normally requires. If, for example, a scene calls for f/8 at 1/125 sec. the two parts of the scene should each be taken at f/11 and 1/125 or f/8 and 1/250 sec. Of course, this rule can be sidestepped for experimental or artistic purposes, but if you want a properly exposed double exposure you should follow it. Another exception to this rule is when images don't overlap . . . as with a dark background (either an area in deep shade or the studio photographer's traditional black velvet). In such instances, "straight" meter readings can be used. Two images are not necessarily better than one but they should be the result of a calculated plan rather than the result of a mistake.

STILL LIFE PHOTOGRAPHY

Serious discussions concerning the emergence of photography as an art form always seem to gravitate toward a comparison of this activity with the ancient art of painting. We do not intend to get involved in this bit of byplay at the moment, except to point out the one big similarity in pursuing both crafts—the attempt to record people and objects permanently. In its early days photography was concentrated on recording subjects realistically and objectively, whereas painting could, and did, wander off into fields of subjective interpretation. Where the former was limited to the "great outdoors" for subject matter, the latter could move into the studio to portray inanimate, and often commonplace, objects. The still life painting thus became a standard production in the artist's repertoire.

In the mid-20th Century, photography has established itself as an art in its own right. The need to compete with painting no longer exists. Having won the "realistic" battle, photographers have been turning to more subjective ways of expressing themselves on film. One means to that end has become the still life photograph. As in painting, the still life on film is generally done completely in the studio. Everything —subject, lighting, recording equipment—is controlled by the photographer. For this reason it may very well be the photographer's purest and most personal form of expression. Ever since Edward Weston's striking rendition of a green pepper, made in the 30's, still life has taken a rightful place alongside the other examples of the photographic

art. It deservedly takes its place within this book, along with other types of great photography.

Choosing a subject for a still life photograph is a personal matter and the choice is bounded only by the

photographer's imagination and the materials at hand. Choosing the equipment for taking these pictures, however, is a more prosaic task. Although some special equipment is ideally suited for still life shooting, you can use existing equipment for the purpose, frequently without extensive adaptation. To some extent, still life photography is equivalent to close-up photography. Though it is not necessarily needed, close-up equipment enables you to photograph still life subjects in great detail and at high magnifications. The bane of close-up photography is blur, resulting from subject movement. But a still life subject does not move and the equipment set-up is thus ideal.

To shoot close-ups you should have an slr camera with interchangeable lenses. Although you can get by with a fixed lens camera, as we will

see, the interchangeable le slr provides much more versc ity. Close-up equipment is re quired to extend the lens awa from the body so that it will b able to focus on an object close range, thereby providi an enlarged detailed image a small area. As with any oth piece of accessory equipme close-up devices require ad justments in the actual pictu taking and we will take them as we go along.

The simplest form of close-equipment does not require lens interchangeability. The lens remains on camera in it normal position, the special accessory you add is an au iliary, or supplementary, lens fits right over the end of you normal lens. Available in sta dard threaded versions, it screws into the inner rim of t front edge of the camera ler They come in various strengt (example: 0, +1 or +2) and, depending on the focal leng of the lens on which they are used, magnify the subject frc about 1/7X to about 2/3X. Whi altering the focal length of t standard lens, they have virt ally no effect on the lens ape ture and, therefore, no expo-sure compensation is neede

For interchangeable lenses, you may use either the auxiliary lenses or an extension ring—a hollow barrel the same diameter as the lens mount—that fits between camera and lens, thus extending the lens for its magnification purposes. Extension rings come in sets of varying lengths. Used singly, or in various combinations, they provide object magnifications from about 1/3X to a full 2X, depending again, on the focal length of the lens. Since they do move the lens farther away from the film, the light passing through must travel a greater distance to the film and a compensation in exposure is necessary. There are instructions and formulas that give you the compensation information, but they are superflous with today's through-lens metering cameras. After some preparatory settings outlined in the manufacturer's instruction book you merely proceed to set exposure as you do in conventional shooting. Even more inviting is the prospect of close-up photography with an electronic

shutter automatic exposure camera with which you simply preset an f stop and press the shutter release. The camera selects the correct shutter speed. Since the f stop and resultant depth-of-field are more important than the shutter speed in still life photography such cameras are ideal.

Closely related to the extension ring method is the bellows extension, a collapsing bellows that fits on camera and can be extended to a greater distance than is possible with rings. In addition, the bellows can be extended to an infinite number of positions out to its maximum and is, thus, more flexible and capable of more precise settings than are the rings. Magnification, with a normal lens, ranges from about .5X to 4X. Exposure setting and compen-

sation are carried out the same as with extension rings.

It is also possible, by means of a special adapter ring, to reverse your normal lens, that is attach its front to the body of your camera or bellows front, for even higher magnifications up to about 9X depending on

the lens. Most convenient of all is the micro lens, an otherwise standard focal length lens with an extended focusing mechanism that permits up to 1/2X magnification with no additional equipment or extraordinary procedures. With a special extension ring, the micro lens can provide life-size (1X) magnification.

This completes the list of special optical equipment needed for close-up still life photography. If you prefer, you can use existing, standard lenses, thereby saving yourself the need to learn a whole new shooting technique. However, you still have to adjust your methods, even with standard equipment. Most normal (50 to 58mm) focal length lenses have a minimum focusing distance of about 18 inches, most wide-angle lenses go down to about 12 inches. Jerry Sarapochiello, whose entire contribution to this book is in the form of still life photographs, suggests the use of normal and shorter focal length lenses because of their ability to render a close-up subject in its more natural, rounded state. Longer focal length and telephoto lenses will flatten out perspective and compress the entire field included in the image. The shorter lenses also provide a greater depth-of-field at a given magnification giving you a better chance of achieving sharp focus over the entire subject area. While the working distance of these short focal length lenses, by themselves, is not adequate for extreme close-up photographs, it is sufficient for still lifes such as those of Sarapochiello.

Lighting of still lifes does not require too much adjustment,

STILL LIFE PHOTOGRAPHY

as relatively standard items are used. Conventional photoflood lamps are best geared for such studio work, partly because of their versatility and simplicity and partly because they are intended for use with tungsten (Type A and B) transparency films. Window and other natural lighting can also be effective. Daylight films can also be used for still lifes with electronic flash but you should use a small unit that is not too powerful. Some of the modern automatic flash units are designed for use at distances between 1 and 2 feet. An electronic ring flash, a doughnut shaped unit that fits around the lens, is well suited for close-up work as it minimizes shadows and is specifically intended for such shooting by emitting a comparatively small amount of light.

The subject matter for still life photography is virtually unlimited. You can follow the lead of the great painters and photograph bowls of fruit, flowers, or a single object such as a vase or other small item. Jerry Sarapochiello, a prime practitioner of this art, prefers to work with odd items he finds or receives from friends. He then may purchase another item to round out his subject. By following his several examples on these pages, we can get a good idea of what he likes to photograph as well as an informative study of the procedures involved.

Sarapochiello's first effort, the double exposure on page 80, was placed on a table with a plexiglas top and illuminated from underneath. Since he was using Type A film, he relied on 3400° K photoflood lamps. The diffused lighting from below enabled his normal micro lens

to register the delicate tracery of the insect's wings. The combined doll's eye and rope was lighted by just one floodlight in a simple reflector from the side, again with the 55mm micro lens. For the sandal on the sand (page 82), Sarapochiello brought his own sand into his studio and arranged it in a beach-like pattern to offset the

haphazard pattern of cracks in the sandal. Once again, a single light was aimed through a diffusing material to cut down its strength and provide a modeling effect for the sand. A wide-angle (28mm) lens provided the necessary sweep to the curving "beach." For the still life on pages 83 and 84, consisting of glass eyes on a piece of wood, Sarapochiello wanted a flatter perspective so he resorted to a 135mm lens with an auxiliary close-up lens. For all still lifes, he suggests keeping the arrangement as simple as possible. Sometimes he makes a preliminary sketch, but simplicity is always his watchword.

Although the examples in this volume do not show it, there is the possibility of some distortion if short focal length lenses are

used by themselves at too close a focusing distance. There are ways, however, to circumvent this. Some 35mm still life photographers use a bellows with a movable front for their close work. The swing and shift movements on this unit give them controls similar to those found on large view cameras. Thus, by adjusting the front of the bellows he can correct the undesirable perspectives that might otherwise occur, and achieve better sharpness control. Another solution is to use a perspective control lens which is available for 35mm cameras and has its own view-camera like movements incorporated into its mechanism.

As with other kinds of photography, the equipment is not a fixed matter. You can rely on standard items or invest in a more complete system. Your subjects can also be standard items or complex, involved, off-beat combinations of flotsam and jetsam. But, whether you take the route of the old masters of painting, or the come-what-may approach of Sarapochiello, the taking of still life photographs is still a challenge to your artistic vision and your photographic skills. By pursuing this type of photography you serve to sharpen your expertise in both areas. Like the great painters, perfecting the still life is an effective way to perfect the overall performance of your craft.

Filters have been in use for ite a long time now and any a photographer has sal- iged his picture by using the ht one in a tricky lighting situ- ion. These small circles of plored glass were originally nd still are) designed for cor- ctive purposes, bringing the rious elements, namely the n and the light source, into alance so that the final iotograph looks natural. obably the most common ample of this balancing act he use of an 85B filter to con- rt a Type B transparency film, rmally balanced for 3200°K igsten light, for use with the 00°K of daylight or electronic sh.) In recent years, however, ere has been a trend toward the use of filters for creative purposes.

The advancement and technological perfection of photographic equipment today has made it virtually im- possible for any competent photographer not to be able to take pictures under most cir- cumstances. This has caused the restless and combative photographer to direct his creative esthetic energies in all sorts of unlikely directions. This book, which presents the work of 17 of these top notch artists, graphically shows some of the best results that can be at- tained with these unconven- tional techniques. No less than 10 of the 17 have chosen un- usual filtration as their vehicle to

artistic creation.

That high proportion should come as no surprise. The in- vestment in filters is relatively small, the portability and maintenance is minimal, and the actual use of them is among the easiest acts in all of pho- tography—you merely attach the filter to the front of your lens. The only requirement is that you know which filters will do what to which films. Once that is mas- tered, and it is a concept simply grasped, there is virtually no limit to the striking and interest- ing effects to be achieved.

We will discuss creative filtra- tion with regard to color film, specifically slides, but the tech- nique is not restricted solely to filters for color film. As you can

Filtration

see from Ken Biggs's stalks of new wheat on pages 11 and 12 a filter normally intended for black-and-white film (here a medium yellow Y48) can be a valuable asset in getting the photographer's particular point across. Before listing the various filters and their original corrective purposes, a brief look at the mechanics involved is in order.

There are basically three ways to attach a glass filter to a lens, two of which require separate adapters. The simplest adapter is a set of plain rings that hold the filter inside and have an external set screw that holds the adapter to the outer rim of the lens. More versatile is the series system, involving a retaining ring that threads into any one of several rings that in turn screw directly into the thread mount at the inner edge of the lens rim. The several rings that make up a series are made for lens diameters within a range of 10 or so mm, but all take the same size filter. Thus you can purchase just one filter with several adapter rings for a set number of different size lenses, this selection is required only if you have lenses with various thread mounts.

Most convenient and permanent are the one-piece self-contained filters with one threaded edge that is made for a specific lens. They will, however, fit into any lens with the same size diameter, such as 52mm, for example.

Filters are no place to economize. They are, after all, in the image path; a poor filter on the front of a good lens results in a poor image. A good filter is of true optical quality.

Somewhat less expensive but more cumbersome are the gelatin filters — square sheets of plastic-like filter material that fit into square metal frames that attach to the lens via the set screw method. They are used primarily with large diameter lenses whose size makes the price of glass filters prohibitive, or when an unusual filter is required — the selection of gelatins is larger.

Black-and-white filters fall into four main categories: yellow, orange, red and green. Yellow filters, further, are available in three grades — light, medium and deep — and green in light and deep gradations. By absorbing ultraviolet, violet and blue light the yellow filter serves to add contrast to sky scenes, so that the clouds stand out clearly. In addition, you can also use light yellow filters for more natural skin tones in outdoor portraits (based on the spectral sensitivity of individual black and white emulsions). As noted before, Biggs used a medium yellow filter to dramatize the out-of-focus background sun in his advertising shot.

Orange filters add emphasis to subjects containing orange, red or yellow and are suitable for detailed landscapes. Red filters are best for heightening contrast and clarity of distant scenic shots and for adding drama and creating a night time effect in sky scenes. Green, by absorbing red, blue and ultraviolet serves mainly to lighten foliage and is also suitable for outdoor portraits. Of course, all four types when used with color film cast their own particular color over the entire scene.

Two types of filters, the skylight and the ultraviolet (UV), can be used with both b&w and color films. Their effect is the least noticeable but nevertheless important. T former cuts down haze and duces the bluish cast of dist landscapes, open shade scenes and pictures made high altitudes. The UV filter do much the same thing but at higher level of efficiency. Interestingly, both of these filte require no exposure compe sation, a factor which we w discuss in greater detail shor

Color film filters fall into thre categories. The best known the conversion filters mention earlier — the 85 series which converts tungsten type films daylight and the 80 series which reverses the procedur For creative filtration purpos the 85 or A Type filters are amber tinted and the 80 or Type filters fall into the blue fa ily. Somewhat similar in purpc are the 81 and 82 series ligh balancing filters that correc minor discrepancies in light sources to achieve the prop balance for films demandin 3200°K or 3400°K color temp ature. Again for creative pu poses, the 81 filters are yellov cast, the 82 filters are blue.

The third category includ the color compensating (C filters intended for correcting overall color cast of a scen compensating for unusually unnatural qualitites of light, such as the excessive greer quality of fluorescent lightin CC filters come in various strengths (designated 10, 2C 30, etc.) in a half dozen col Those colors, with the colors they absorb listed in parenthesis, are: red (blue, greer green (blue, red), blue (rec green), yellow (blue), mage (green) and cyan (red). The can be used singly or in con nation (of the same color o to produce different grade

mpensation as the subject
emands.

Polarizing filters have no
actical effect on the color
alance of your pictures. Their
ain function is to cut down
nd/or eliminate excessive
are in the manner of Polaroid®
nglasses. They also darken
es and intensify color satu-
tion with the reduction of
are. John Lawlor's figure
dy on page 52 and Richard
eedman's multiple print of a
ndscape on pages 89 and 90
ustrate the effective use of a
olarizing filter. Steedman re-
d on it to bring out the details
his landscape at sunset,
dded the conventional moon
ot afterward in the darkroom.

Another filter with no effect
color, the neutral density fil-
r, is supplied in various grades
nd is used to cut down on the
ength of the light source,
ermitting, for example, the use
a very fast film in an excep-
nally bright light. George
oremski relied on a neutral
ensity filter to reduce the ex-
osure of his multiple view of
otre Dame (page 75). Be-
ause it freed him from the
ecessity of changing aperture
ter each shot, he was able to
ke his multiple views in rapid
ccession, moving nothing but
camera for each shot.

ll of these filters, with the ex-
eption of skylight and ultra-
olet, require some compen-
tion in exposure setting. De-
ending on the strength of the
er the compensation varies
m about 1/2 to more than
ee full f/stops. The exact de-
ee of compensation is clearly
arked in the filter's instruction
eet and, in many cases, with
data sheet supplied with
film. However, the advent of
behind-the-lens meter has

made these filter factor instructions basically obsolete. In fact,
these meters make creative use
of filters more practical since
they measure the light passing
through the filter to the film.

There are, of course, as many
creative filtration possibilities as
there are film and filter combinations, a virtually limitless
number. Perhaps as a start you
can follow the lead of Pete
Turner who frequently uses an
indoor film (Type A) outdoors,
thereby creating an enriched
blue cast while playing down
the warmer reds and oranges
of his subject. He carried this
cooling effect a step farther in
photographing the Icelandic
volcano (pages 95 and 96) by
adding a CC blue filter. The
same combination was used
to reiterate the overall blue
of the underground church
scene on page 93, creating
an exaggerated sense of
the subterranean.

Other possibilities, similar to
the technique of Biggs and his
yellow filter, are apparent in the
work of Mitchell Funk who
added blue to deepen the existing blue of his multiple exposure on pages 29 and 30, Tom
McCarthy who added a deep
red filter to an early morning
scene (page 64) to get the
sun at the right angle, and
Meola's use of an orange filter
to express the domination of the
sun in his scene on page 68.

For a textbook example of
the value of a skylight filter at
higher elevations see Henry
Wolf's snow-covered Swiss
mountain scene on page 101. In
case you doubt the prepon-
derance of blue in such scenes,
Wolf's picture should prove
convincing. The filter, here,
helped him realize the great
amount of detail apparent in

the scene. Likewise, Anthony
Edgeworth's reliance on a
polarizing filter darkened the
sky and created the contrast
that makes the picture of
Brasilia found on pages 23-24.

You can try combining
special picture-making techniques, such as multiple exposures of a moving subject,
with each picture taken
through a different colored filter
for a multi-colored animation
effect.

These are but a few of the
directions you can follow. The
mechanical aspects are easily
overcome. If you have several
lenses with different focal
lengths but with the same
diameter, so much the better
for your investment. The technical aspects have also been
taken care of by your camera.
All that remains to solve is the
creative aspect. Here you are
limited only by your imagination. For a start you can hold the
filter, by itself, up to your eye
and observe how the world
looks through colored glasses.
For the particular effect of one
filter on one film you may have
to wait a while until your film is
processed. In other cases you
should be able to predict the
results. You may wind up with a
world that is not right in the eyes
of the purist and the conformist,
but it will be an infinitely more
beautiful and interesting world
— a world that you, yourself,
have created.

SLIDE COPYING

A good picture may well be worth the proverbial 1000 words but that doesn't mean it can't be made even better. This is particularly true when considering the 35mm slide, which is rapidly becoming the most popular form of expression of pictorial subjects. Indeed, this book is living proof of the acceptance and capabilities of the slide as a means of portraying a variety of subjects — from striking landscapes to intimate personal studies.

Good as they are, however, there are times when slides can be improved. This fact, together with the few times when slides are less than satisfactory but still salvageable, has led to a practice which can best be described as slide manipulation. There are several ways to alter a slide and there are several reasons for doing it. Some slides may be perfectly composed, capturing just the right moment, but poorly exposed. Others may be technically satisfactory but lacking in some bit of subject detail, such as having too much sky overpowering an otherwise pleasant landscape. There are also many kinds of special effects the photographer might want to use to depict a subject in a highly personal artistic fashion. And, finally, there are purely abstract designs and patterns which can only be recorded photographically by manipulation of the materials (ordinary slides) at hand.

Perhaps the most widely known method of altering slides is the technique known as the sandwich, in which two or more slides are combined into a single mount and then rephotographed (copied) to create a new "original" image. The sandwich material may be

a second slide with an augmenting subject, a plain piece of colored material that serves as a background, or even a black-and-white copy of the same or another slide. The effect can be quite similar to that of a multiple exposure, but since the technique of producing them differs greatly, we will discuss that method elsewhere.

The usual procedure is to open the standard cardboard slide mount, remove the film itself, arrange the various pieces as desired and then bind the entire sandwich in a glass or plastic mount. These special mounts come in various forms. Some of the plastic mounts are snapped together to hold the sandwich in place. Others rely on thin metal frames into which the entire sandwich is inserted. In any case, the glass or plastic mount is preferable to the cardboard variety. There are many of the latter which employ a heat sealing technique. After the sandwich has been inserted you tack the mount closed with the tip of a heated flatiron.

To obtain a multiple series of repeating images, such as the Danish Palace guard by George Obremski on page 74,

you can make several cop of the original image and th mount the entire series in a sandwich. The copying proc itself is, therefore, crucial to entire alteration process. On again, there are several methods of copying slides, ranging from a sophisticate self-contained professional copier to a do-it-yourself co bination of various standar accessories used in conjun tion with a few home remed

To begin with, you can ma slide copies with your present camera and normal le provided, of course, that th lens can be removed and tended from the body. The cial factor in the procedure i move the lens far enough aw from the film plane so that it c focus on the subject — the sl being copied — at close ran and produce a 1:1, or same size, image copy of that su ject. A good rule of thumb requires a distance equal t the focal length of the lens same size copying, which t necessitates a compensatic the exposure setting of two f/stops. More about that la

The subject slide, in turn, n be placed the same distar from the front of the lens as film plane is from the rear of lens. There are several devi made for extending the ler away from the camera bo (also intended for conventic close-up photography) as v as items for holding the slide the proper distance (their s purpose and use).

The least expensive way copy a slide is with your camera's normal lens. It can positioned the required dis tance by either of two acc sories. The most basic is a se extension tubes (also calle rings) which are hollow lens I

that fit into the camera
dy. (Naturally, they must
ve the same type mount as
 camera on which they are
 d.) The one drawback of
se tubes is that they are of a
 d length. But they do come
 sets of varying lengths. By
 ng one or more of the tubes in
 rious combinations it is pos-
 le to obtain the desired ex-
 sion, the combination being
 result of either trial and error
 precise calculation. Then,
 en the rigid nature of the
 es, it is possible that you may
 ver actually get the exact ex-
 sion required.

On the other hand, the exten-
 n bellows is a much more
 ible and precise copying
 l. It consists of a collapsible
 lows, on a track, which can
 racked out to an infinite
 mber of continuously vari-
 le distances. The bellows is
 turally more expensive than
 ube set and is ideally suited
 use with a micro or short
 al length (24 to 85mm) lens.
 he simplest, and best, meth-
 is with a micro or close-
 using lens. The extended
 using ability of such lenses
 ally permits making a 1:2,
 alf-life-size, copy. However,
 st "micro" lenses are sup-
 ed with a special adapter
 t fits between the lens and
 mera, thus extending the
 s farther from the film and
 king a 1:1 copy possible.
 Final member of the copying
 m is a slide copy device to
 d the slide being copied.
 most effective slide copy-
 devices can be attached to
 front of a bellows mount. As
 n the bellows separating the
 s from the camera, bellows-
 e slide holders are more
 cise and flexible than the
 d variety. The slide copy de-
 itself consists of a position-

ing gate with a diffusion glass to
allow illumination. In addition to
positioning the slide properly,
some slide copy devices offer
other advantages such as
movements in both directions
for critical positioning. Such
movements permit centering of
the slide for copies greater than
1:1 or for "cropping".

By adjusting the controls
governing the distances on
either side of the lens (with tubes
or bellows) you control the
magnification, focusing and
subject matter of your copy. But
you still need a light source. A
photoflood lamp or flash unit
(electronic is preferable to the
bulb type) mounted on a
tripod, behind the slide will fill
the bill nicely. Optimum distance between light and slide is
1-2 feet. With a flood lamp or
other continuous light source
you can obtain the proper
exposure settings with your
camera's behind-the-lens
meter, much the same as in
normal shooting. An automatic
exposure camera makes the
procedure even easier.

There is more calculation required with flash inasmuch as
each light source and distance
differ so widely. The calculation, however, involves the
standard guide number procedure used in ordinary flash
shooting. Divide the distance
between flash unit and slide
copying device into the guide
number for the film in use to get
the "normal" aperture. Then
open your lens approximately 2
stops for diffusion screen plus
bellows extension compen-
sation. This gives you a good
starting point but you should
bracket exposures, shooting as
many as 10 different pictures at
half stop intervals. You should
record all the data so that you
can discern the best aperture

for that particular slide-lens-
light setup. Use it for subsequent
copies. The aperture will, by
and large, be satisfactory for all
other slides of like density. For
other slides, you'll have to adjust your basic aperture up or
down as needed if you wish to
compensate (lighten or dark-
en). To be sure, bracket again
two or three half-stops in the
direction you wish to compensate. (This procedure should
also be followed for continuous
light copying.)

Most slide copies, no matter
what film or light source, tend to
be too contrasty. You can
reduce this contrast through
a technique known as pre-flash-
ing, in which you expose the
film to an even, low-level
light (ideally the same light to
be used for the actual copy,
screened by an ND 2.0 gelatin
filter) before you make the
copy. Your camera must have
provision for making double
exposures. The first exposure will
be the flashed exposure; the
second, the actual copy.

Professional type slide
copiers come complete with
light source. With most you can
use your own camera and lens,
but one unit supplies even
those items. All you need do is
insert slide and copying film,
compose, focus and shoot.
The investment in this piece of
equipment is so great that only
those photographers planning
production work in which they
will copy a great many slides
over the years will even consider buying it.

You don't need a special film
for slide copying, although
there are several emulsions
available just for that purpose.
With a daylight source, such as
electronic flash, you can use
your favorite transparency film.
Another good combination is a

SLIDE COPYING

Type A film with a photoflood lamp. Among the special duplicating films are Kodak's Ektachrome Reversal Print Film 5038, balanced for 3200°K (quartz lamp) and GAF's Anscochrome 5470, balanced for 3000°K. You may want to add a UV filter and/or color compensating filters to get the copy just to your requirements. These films come in 100-foot rolls and must be respooled onto reusable cassettes.

We mentioned the series of repeating images as one possible sandwich. Another is the overlay, rather the underlay, of a piece of film or plastic of a certain color to change the overall tone of the slide which may be woefully overexposed or otherwise in need of correction and/or enhancing. For example, a blue overall background will restore the natural coloring of a washed out seascape or landscape. Still other scenes might be improved with the addition of the sun or moon or stars. A void can be filled with such as a lone tree. Then there are all the trick and gag shots that can result from a skillful pairing of two different images.

For these reasons it's a good idea to stock your photographic larder with a good supply of sandwich making materials. For example, if you come across a particularly photogenic moon, you should photograph it many times, perhaps devoting an entire roll of film to it, which can then be stored. When the need arises, you can go to your "moon bank" and insert a moon slide into a sandwich. Or you can keep just one "perfect" moon shot on file as a master. When and as you have a slide crying out for just such a sandwich

partner, you can easily make a copy of the master or use the master in the final printing of the sandwich.

Everyone likes to be perfect the first time out, especially with slides. The sandwich technique, however, can help improve imperfect slides, and sometimes make good ones even better — after the fact. It's easier than you think, requiring only an

extra piece of equipment o two. It's likely that you have n of the ingredients already. effort involved is not strenuc and is definitely rewarding. You'll realize that when you cover you won't have to gc back to the scene and shoc over again. You can't dupl cate conditions of nature, k you can manipulate them conform to your memory.